MW00680794

grow the %*@# up

grow the %*@# up

how to be an adult and get treated like one

SARAH KNIGHT

VORACIOUS

Little, Brown and Company

New York   Boston   London

Voracious / Little, Brown and Company
Hachette Book Group
1290 Avenue of the Americas, New York, NY 10104
voraciousbooks.com

First Edition: April 2023

Voracious is an imprint of Little, Brown and Company, a division of Hachette Book Group, Inc. The Voracious name and logo are trademarks of Hachette Book Group, Inc.

The publisher is not responsible for websites (or their content) that are not owned by the publisher.

The Hachette Speakers Bureau provides a wide range of authors for speaking events. To find out more, go to hachettespeakersbureau.com or email HachetteSpeakers@hbgusa.com.

Little, Brown and Company books may be purchased in bulk for business, educational, or promotional use. For information, please contact your local bookseller or the Hachette Book Group Special Markets Department at special.markets@hbgusa.com.

Illustrations and hand-lettering by Lauren Harms

ISBN 9780316473224 (HC) / 9780316567657 (clean cover edition)
LCCN 2022951276

Printing 1, 2023

LSC-C

Printed in the United States of America

For Robert Ray Knight

You're going to learn the F-word someday, kid.

It might as well be from me.

Contents

It's grow time! **3**

    Growing pains? More like growing *GAINS*. **8**

    Oh yeah? You're not my mom! **9**

    The GTFU MO **13**

        Feat. Maturity, responsibility, accountability **17**

    Because I said so **19**

PUTTING THE "FUN" IN FUNDAMENTALS:
Basic bits and starter tips to get you in the grownup
groove **23**

    The evolution of a Total Fucking Grownup **26**

        Actual Babies, Big Fucking Babies, Theoretical Adults, and Total
        Fucking Grownups **27**

    Finish your chores and you can go play **33**

        GTFU MO-tivation: Reward and Relief (R&R) **34**

        Learning your ABCs **38**

You know better than that **38**

    Feat. Consequences **40**

    Anticipate & Orchestrate **41**

The C-Cycle **45**

    Critical Thinking **46**

    Communication **48**

    Coping **51**

Noooo! I don't *wanna!* **55**

    Feat. Habits and incentives **56**

    Brush your teeth **56**

        Optimize **57**

        Solve for X **58**

        Make sucky things suck less **59**

        How to form a habit in 3 easy steps **62**

    Here, have a lollipop! **64**

        Difficult or annoying shit I have to deal with:
            An exercise **67**

Secret Bonus C: Confidence **68**

Am I acting like a fucking adult? (A flowchart) **71**

FOR MATURE AUDIENCES ONLY: Self-awareness, self-control, and being on your best adult behavior **73**

Self-awareness **77**

    Do you have something to tell me? **78**

The HOW/WHY/WHAT Method for figuring it out, so you can spit it out   **80**

Be your own Bad Cop   **88**

Talking the talk AND walking the walk   **89**

Look both ways   **92**

Self-control   **98**

Mind your manners   **99**

Feat. The Golden Rule   **100**

6 Extra-Impressive and Equally Easy Ways to Be Polite, Beyond Saying *Please* and *Thank you*   **104**

Be quiet   **104**

Bite your tongue   **105**

Be complimentary   **107**

"My lord, that ass!"   **108**

Be diplomatic   **109**

What you're thinking / What you could say instead   **109**

Be considerate   **110**

Be kind   **112**

Don't you take that tone with me   **113**

The calm before the tweetstorm   **114**

No fussin'   **116**

Put yourself in "time-out"   **117**

The Triple O   **118**

Just fucking let it go   **122**

Feat. The One Question to Rule Them All   **122**

5 ways to let it go   **123**

Stand up straight, and no fidgeting   **124**

Take a deep breath   **124**

Strike a Power Pose   **125**

Dress for success **126**

Use your words **127**

Do you kiss Beyoncé with that mouth? **129**

I'll give you something to whine about **131**

What if it's not them, it's you? **135**

PS: Read the room **135**

I thought I asked you not to do that **136**

Boundary / How to respect it **139**

WITH GREAT RESPONSIBILITY COMES GREAT POWER: The perks of being independent and dependable, and how to get there **143**

A GYST-claimer **146**

Independence (taking on responsibility) **147**

If everybody else jumped off a bridge, would you do it too? **148**

Feat. Prioritizing (the "making choices based on your values" kind) **148**

What do I value?: An exercise **150**

Decisions, decisions **152**

Mommy needs a minute **157**

Just do it. (Yourself.) **161**

Doing X / Gets you Y **163**

Help! **166**

Are you sure you looked everywhere? **166**

3 questions resourceful people ask themselves on the reg **169**

Make believe and make it work: An exercise **171**

Eat your vegetables **174**

5 benefits of taking responsibility for your health apart from the actual health benefits **175**

TIP THE FIRST: There is no one-size-fits-all prescription for feelin' your best **175**

Sleep it off **177**

Get it on **177**

You booze, you lose? **178**

I feel better when / I feel like shit when: An exercise **180**

Ew, gross! **181**

TIP THE SECOND: Ignore the noise **181**

TIP THE THIRD: Get yourself a doctor. And then actually go see them. **183**

Wear a helmet **186**

Go pro **187**

Run, don't walk **188**

Don't beat yourself up **189**

But do listen *up* **190**

Dependability (acting responsibly) **192**

Maybe you should have thought of that before we left the house **193**

3 tips for becoming a Totally Fucking Dependable Total Fucking Grownup **195**

Don't overcommit **195**

Spell it out (set *expectations*) **196**

Rein it in (manage *expectations*) **197**

5 things you get by being totally fucking dependable **200**

3 more trusty tips to help you go from "Haha, I'm not much of a planner!" to "No worries, I'm on it!" **200**

'Twas the night before I had shit to do   **200**

Take the long view   **201**

Put it in writing   **202**

Find your shoes, it's time to go!   **204**

How long is this gonna take?   **205**

Planning is cool, but have you tried execution?   **207**

Feat. Prioritizing ("the getting on task and staying there" kind)   **207**

The Must-Do Method   **208**

The MDM 2.0   **209**

Do your homework   **211**

5 ways to do your homework   **212**

Money doesn't grow on trees   **214**

Budgeting   **216**

Saving   **219**

When taxes attack!   **221**

A whole other level of adult financial fun   **222**

IV

SORRY, MY BAD: Owning up to what you did and stepping up to fix it   225

Owning up   **229**

Come on, don't be like that   **230**

3 tips for defusing your defense mechanisms   **233**

Listen to judgment without judgment   **233**

You're in this together   **234**

Two things can be true AT THE SAME TIME **234**

Who let the dog out? **237**

Liar, Liar: Thing you fucked up / Don't say / Do say **239**

Master Equivocator: Thing you fucked up / Don't say / Do say **240**

Is this a *reasonable* reason? **241**

Unreasonable reasons for why you fucked up **242**

Apologize to your sister! **243**

Way to apologize / Potential add-on **245**

Sorry, NotSorry **247**

Stepping up **249**

Go clean your room **250**

6 tips for keeping your actual room clean, because I cannot help myself **254**

The most effective way to 'fess up AND step up **254**

Did you learn your lesson? **256**

Check your work **256**

It's as easy as C, B, A **258**

Feat. The Reverse ABC **258**

EPILOGUE: Everybody try! **263**

Acknowledgments **271**

Index **275**

About the Author **285**

grow
the
%*@#
up

It's grow time!

One cool thing about being an adult is that it is *the* single common goal shared by every baby ever born, which means we are truly all in this together. And even cooler? Everyone you know is rooting for you to ROCK IT.

Your parents, grandparents, teachers, and coaches have always wanted to see you thrive, and your friends have been cheering from the sidelines as you hit grownup milestones together — from getting driver's licenses and jobs to potentially coupling up and settling down to one day maybe watching your kids rock it together too. (Or if you're like me, watching your friends' kids from afar, while you sip a margarita at the adults-only pool.)

It's exciting stuff, growing up! It can also be intimidating, given that gaining entry to the land of adult privileges and beverages requires you to be able to think for yourself and support yourself and take care of yourself largely independent of the network that carried you this far. Those folks won't spontaneously combust the day you legally divest from childhood, but they've got plenty of their own exciting/intimidating stuff to deal with, so at a certain point you've got to get comfortable handling your grownup shit your grownup *self*.

And it works both ways. As much as your loved ones want YOU to be stable and happy and on time for dinner, you want the same for (and from) them. Your coworkers depend on you to pull your weight, and you, theirs. Your neighbors look to you to be a respectful member of the community, and you, right back at 'em. And the person working the deli counter during the lunch rush sure would appreciate it if you know your order when you get to the front of the line — just like you'll appreciate it when they get your sandwich right.

Like I said, we're all in this together, so we ALL benefit from leading by example.

This book will help you be the grownup you want to see in the world. And while it does not contain step-by-step instructions for changing the fluid in your windshield wipers or filing your taxes (sorry, that's on you), it does show you how to develop the skills and master the mind-set that make you the kind of person who understands *why* they need to do that kind of stuff and who is more than capable of figuring it out.

For themselves.

Like an adult.

Which is pretty cool.

* * *

So let's start with you, kiddo. (Can I call you kiddo? It has such a jaunty ring to it.) What brought you to the opening pages of a sweary little book about growing the fuck up?

Perhaps you're **an industrious young person seeking a head start on facing and embracing the wide adult world.** If so, that's awesome and I am here for it. (And if you're a parent hunting for the perfect graduation gift for said young person, I promise they'll be in good hands.)

Maybe you're only **recently out on your own and beginning to wish you'd paid more attention in the Before Times** — back when magic elves stocked the cupboards with cereal and folded your laundry and offered wise counsel on breakups and bad days. That was nice, huh?

Then again, maybe you **didn't have great role models/magic elves** growing up, and there wasn't much to pay attention *to* in the teaching and coaching and handholding departments. If **circumstances forced you into adulthood unprepared** and you've been scrambling ever since, know that I am sympathetic to your struggles and confident we can leave them in the rearview.

Or hey, perhaps **you've been at this for quite some time indeed...and getting mixed results.** Experiencing more bad days than good ones lately, leading to waning confidence in your grownup prowess? No worries, it happens to the best of us! We'll get you back on track, Boomer.

In any case, I'm delighted to say you've come to the right place — because I've designed *Grow the Fuck Up* for **ANYONE** who needs **ANY HELP** at **ANY AGE** in getting their adulting game up to snuff.

It's for **precocious teens** and **recent grads** and **twentysome-things** who may have moved out of Mom and Dad's blast radius but are still clinging to the credit cards, phone plan, and Netflix account.

It's for **twenty-nine- and thirty-five- and forty-one-year-olds** who are surviving, if not necessarily thriving; aka **Elder Millennials and Gen-X'ers** who could use a refresher course in Adulting 101 (and who'll appreciate all of my nineties pop culture references, as a treat).

And it's for **midlife meanderers** and **pre- and post-retirees,** because WHY THE FUCK NOT.* I don't want anybody to

---

* *Why the Fuck Not?* is the book I plan to write when I'm eighty years old and enjoying my Wednesdays with a glass of Pinot and a cannabis lollipop at a darling little cat café in the Eleventh Arrondissement. Stay tuned.

feel left out just because they have to scroll for thirty seconds to find their birth year in a dropdown menu.

It's never too late to acquire (or revive) a bunch of primo life skills. Seriously, who's going to complain if you suddenly become more polite, dependable, self-aware, self-sufficient, and all-around awesome? Not your friends, family, partner, coworkers, or boss, I'd wager. And certainly not yours truly, who would appreciate it if more people of all ages whom she encounters on any given day were a little less irresponsible and a lot more mature. Just sayin'.

And you've made it this far, so let's put all your cards on the table. How often do you think to yourself —

I could have planned for this . . . but I didn't.

I waited for somebody else to take care of it . . . but they didn't.

I am not handling this very well . . . AT ALL.

If the answers are anywhere south of *Never,* then I think you're going to be happy you showed up to this party.

Growing pains? More like growing GAINS.

Making your way in the world — at any age, and especially once nobody else is legally or morally obligated to help you along — can be tricky, no diggity.* But **the _rewards_ of adulting wisely and well are numerous,** and they're worth the effort it takes on your part to unlock now and enjoy forever.

Like, sure, being an adult has its challenges — what with all the bills and jobs and bills and apartment searches and bills and dating apps and bills and jury duty and bills and diaper duty and bills and so on until you die.

Boo!

But adults _also_ get to drive and vote and plan their own vacations and legally order mojitos and stay up late and eat Munchies Nacho Cheese Snack Mix for dinner anytime they goddamn feel like it. And if you stick around long enough to achieve senior citizen status, many societies will see fit to reward you with half-price movie tickets and free refills on iced tea.

Yay!

And the truly _adult_ adults — the responsible, emotionally mature grownups; not just the ones with a minimum of eighteen

---

* '90s children, holla!

years on file — get to enjoy all of that and more. They have healthy relationships and practical skills and good reputations and solid career prospects. They know their way around fancy cheese carts and how to unselfishly pleasure their partners, and they have at least one clean shirt available AT ALL TIMES.

Sorcery!

That's right, folks: this whole adulting gig ain't half bad. Especially when you're *good* at it.

Furthermore, while saying goodbye to the blissful ignorance of your younger years and hello to the responsibilities of growing older might, on its surface, sound like a drag...IT DOESN'T HAVE TO BE. Actually, there are **plenty of sneakily simple ways to make all that adulting EASIER and MORE PLEAS-ANT,** ensuring much smoother sailing on your way to cashing in those early-bird specials.

And I'm going to show you how.

Oh yeah? You're not my mom!

Touché. But I hear ya. You're entitled to ask what qualifies me to be your growing-the-fuck-up guide. And I want you to feel good about our time together, so please allow me to present my bona fides:

In 2015, when I was thirty-six years old, I left my first career as a book editor at a major publishing house in New York City and struck out on my own as a freelancer. I wanted to escape unsavory office politics, be my own boss, and move to a tropical island where I would never again be prevailed upon to wear pants to work. Then (perhaps not surprisingly) I had the idea for my first book, *The Life-Changing Magic of Not Giving a Fuck,* which taught people the art of "mental decluttering" and became a bestseller all over the world. Today I live in the Dominican Republic and have a whole series of sweary self-help books under my belt, a ten-million-view TEDx Talk, and a podcast that reached number one on the Apple Education charts, which was neat.

Along the way, I became known as **"the anti-guru"** and *Elle* magazine once described me as Amy Schumer-meets-Oprah, which should tell you everything you need to know about how I operate.

My No Fucks Given Guides (NFGGs, for short) have helped millions of readers give fewer, better fucks (*The Life-Changing Magic of Not Giving a Fuck*); get organized (*Get Your Shit Together*); embrace their idiosyncrasies (*You Do You*); manage their anxiety (*Calm the Fuck Down*); and set strong boundaries (*Fuck No!*).* And to be honest, I thought about stopping there so I could move on to

---

*Grow the Fuck Up contains a little bit of all of that, but I promise it isn't just a clever way of conning you into paying full price for a half-assed remix. I may have a filthy sense of humor, but I also have my integrity.

my third career as a professional cat lady, but then in 2020 something happened to make me reconsider.

That summer, as luck and months of early-pandemic-era unemployed isolation in a tiny apartment would have it, my brother and sister-in-law announced that they were having a baby. Which meant I was soon to be a first-time aunt.

Well, huh.

I'd been lucky to have a few fabulous aunts of my own growing up, and it felt like a baton was being passed. It got me thinking, *What might I have to offer this next generation of Knight, apart from the requisite hilarious onesies, annual birthday and Christmas gift cards, and starter bongs?*

Here I should note that although I possess what I believe to be a great many worthy notions for encouraging impressionable young humans to flourish as functioning members of adult society — A GREAT MANY — I don't have children of my own, so I've historically avoided sharing those notions with other people's kiddos. Mostly because I understand that it's "not cool" to "offer them unbidden" and I have wished to neither get throat-punched nor excommunicated by my parent friends.

So on the one hand, here was my brother, poised to bring another child into the world that I knew I ought to refrain from backseat parenting. But on the other, well, what good is having a bestselling anti-guru in the family if you can't score first dibs on her best practices for meeting life's various and sundry challenges?

AN *AUNTIE*-GURU, IF YOU WILL.

That's when *Grow the Fuck Up* began to take shape. I figured if I put my adulting advice into a book that was available to *anybody* who *chose* to read it, then *nobody* would have cause to get throat-punchy — and in addition to my nephew, I could help a whole passel of current AND future adults live their best lives. (Plus, my husband is really not into the professional cat lady idea.)

And so, this book was inspired by and is dedicated to one Robert Ray Knight. Although he'll only be two when it comes out, he's *very* advanced for his age, and I trust he'll be flipping through it in no time. Or at least chewing on it.

Meanwhile — and more immediately — I hope it will help YOU navigate adult life with a little more ease, a lot more pleasure, an appreciation for the advantages of critical thinking, a cornucopia of communication and coping skills, and enough motherfucking hangers to keep all of your shirts off the floor.

Seriously, *all* of them. It's just not that hard.

If Auntie Sarah has done her job, then one day soon, neither you nor Robert will need me anymore. You'll be out there

putting your best grown-ass adult feet forward — at home, at work, in your relationships, health, finances, and more — and becoming the architect of your own happiness and success. And then you can pay it forward and help the generation that follows you do the same.

You know, if humanity makes it that far.

Boop.

The GTFU MO

At this point you may be thinking, *Okay, "Auntie Sarah," I'll play along. But what does "being an adult" even* mean?

Good question, and I'm glad to see you're already engaging with the material. Gold star for you! And we'll get there. But first, let's look at some of the responses I received from the anonymous survey I conducted before I sat down to write the book. I do this with all of my NFGGs because it helps me gauge my readers' biggest concerns and focus the material on what you guys need, rather than solely on what *I* feel the need to tell you. (Though there will be plenty of that, too. See: A GREAT MANY NOTIONS.)

Anyway, I think if we run through a few of the Qs and As up front, it'll show you that a) you're not alone in your adulting struggles and b) I'm not just talking out of my ass for the next three hundred pages. My first question was:

What does being an adult mean to YOU?

A majority of responders cited some version of "being responsible" and "being a productive member of society" — specifically mentioning things like managing their finances, caring for loved ones, and serving their communities. Cool, cool.

A large number pointed toward more existential goals, such as "controlling my emotional response," "being a good role model," and "learning to be more mindful of what really matters." Sounds good.

And some answers were more personal and specific (and occasionally hilarious), but nevertheless indicative of the difference between an adult-in-age-only and a true pro- dult — such as "taking vitamins," "raising kids who aren't assholes," and "knowing how to use Saran Wrap without wanting to throw it across the room in a fit of rage." (I'm adding that last one to my own adulting checklist, BTW. Always room to improve.)

My favorite response was this: "Adulting means that when something bad happens, I stop looking around for an adultier adult to fix it." Truly says it all, folks. By the end of this book, I want YOU to be the adultiest adult in the room. (I mean, besides me, of course.)

I also asked questions like these:

Name something your parent/s* taught you that you think really helped you in life.
Integrity and work ethic ranked high; but to the person who said "Nothing, lol, my parents were garbage," I see you, and I am here to help.

What's something your parent/s *didn't* teach you and you wish they had?

Financial responsibility, self-care, mental health care, and relationship skills cropped up often. (And so they shall in part III…)

---

* Note: Throughout *Grow the Fuck Up,* I'll be using terms like "parents," "Mom," and "Dad" to encompass all manner of guardians and authority figures, such as grandparents, teachers, coaches, nuns, babysitters, etc. I understand that not everyone has a standard nuclear family setup, and if that's you, I hope you won't feel left out by my occasional need to generalize for the sake of keeping things snappy.

And just for fun, I asked:

If you are *not* a parent, what's one thing you wish other people would teach their kids?
Manners, kindness, and accountability were leading contenders. Additionally, several survey-ees took this opportunity to lament that children are WAY TOO LOUD, an observation I enthusiastically cosign.

(On that note: I know it can be hard to regulate the tots' internal volume controls, but if I could prevail upon any parents who may be reading to at least not teach said tots to play "Marco Polo" in a public pool, I would consider it a generous gift to me and all of humanity. Thanks a bunch!)

With these and many more terrific insights-slash-cries for help in hand, the next order of business was to organize my findings. And so, my little fucklings, after crunching all the data — also known as "scrolling through a massive Google Form while sitting on my couch eating a bowl of Doritos" — here you have it:
What being an adult even *means* — aka the *modus operandi* of growing the fuck up, henceforth known as the GTFUMO.

THE GTFU MO
MATURITY
+
RESPONSIBILITY
+
ACCOUNTABILITY

In broad strokes, executing the GTFU MO looks like this:

Being MATURE

as in being honest, polite, respectful, gracious, self-aware, etc.
These qualities are behavior-oriented.

Being RESPONSIBLE

as in being self-sufficient and resourceful, planning ahead,
being dependable, etc.
These qualities are action-oriented.

Being ACCOUNTABLE

as in being able to accept criticism, apologize, learn from your mistakes, etc.

These qualities combine **mature behavior** AND **responsible action.**

When you stick to the GTFU MO, you are officially *being* an adult — which creates a virtuous cycle that leads to you **getting** *treated like* an adult, too.

You'll be granted freedom, autonomy, respect, and trust from all those other people in your life who appreciate your efforts to be mature, responsible, and accountable. Yup:

Freedom

Autonomy

Respect

Trust

That's just a little bit of what you stand to gain in exchange for being a mature adult who is definitely not giggling at that acronym.

So now you've got your marching orders, and I'll spend the rest of this book explaining how to follow them, for your own AND everyone else's benefit.

We'll do it by going back to basics … with a twist.

Because I said so

If you took a peek at the table of contents and spotted entries like "Brush your teeth" and "Eat your vegetables," you'd be forgiven for thinking you got tricked into a book-length nag-fest. I ASSURE YOU, YOU DID NOT. The chapter titles are mostly my idea of a fun organizational gimmick — and anyway, I didn't become a bestselling anti/auntie-guru because I don't know how to deliver an intimidating self-improvement regimen with wit and flair. This whole experience will be akin to me sneaking vegetables into your smoothie. (Or onto your pizza, which is more my style.)

I'm just going to use those parental admonitions and decrees as jumping-off points, and then I'll turn them upside down and inside out to reveal the great and glorious practical applications they contain — not only for "not getting grounded" and "being a stand-up citizen of the world" — but for **"getting what YOU want and making YOUR life EASIER and MORE PLEASANT."**

Part I: Putting the "Fun" in FUNdamentals offers a sneak peek at a shitload of grownup perks and a few key tools and strategies for achieving them.

Part II: For Mature Audiences Only shows you how to be on your best adult behavior *and* how to get the most out of it.

Part III: With Great Responsibility Comes Great Power is a guide to all of the practical strategies you could ever need to get shit done and open doors, both personally and professionally.

Then, last but certainly not least —

Part IV: Sorry, My Bad demonstrates various ways of holding yourself accountable, and explains why those are the most essential — and impressive — grownup skills of them all.

And that's just a little preview of where we're headed. By the end of the book, you'll be able to:

- Practice self-awareness and maintain self-control
- Ask for what you want, in a way that makes you more likely to get it

- Orchestrate the best possible outcomes for yourself…
- …and cope with the worst ones
- Use habits and incentives to make adulting easier and more pleasant
- Go from fully dependent to gloriously *in*dependent AND depend*able*
- Slay self-care
- Apologize with aplomb
- And more!

Plus, among all the practical how-tos and the philosophical why-you-should-want-tos, I'll sprinkle in plenty of my best hyper-specific **Pro-dult Tips** for good measure. Auntie Sarah intends to send you out there with confidence, verve, *and* a bottle of Goo Gone to keep under the sink. That shit is MAGIC.

So how about it? Time to put on your game face, bust out those big-kid panties, and grow the fuck up!

It'll be fun. I promise.

1

PUTTING THE "FUN" IN FUNDAMENTALS:

Basic bits and starter tips to get you in the grownup groove

Before we get into the play-by-play for becoming more mature (part II), responsible (part III), and accountable (part IV), there are **a few key concepts** I want to cover that'll get you geared up to grow up like a boss.

First, I'll walk you through **the evolution of adulting** and point out **the differences between Big Fucking Babies and Total Fucking Grownups.** Then I'll help you **find your GTFU MO-tivation** and show you the first of many easy ways to become a TFG, by **learning a new twist on your ABCs.**

After that, we'll move on to **the mother of all guiding principles — CONSEQUENCES —** and a simple way to get them working *for* instead of *against* you. Anticipate! Orchestrate! Checkmate! Then we'll take **a ride on the C-Cycle,** which incorporates three more skills that underlie pretty much every adult action and behavior there is: **critical thinking, communication, and coping.** These buddies are gonna pop up all the way through the book, so get used to 'em.

I'll round out part I with **a pair of uberpractical tips for kicking your adult game into high gear,** and a new entry in my popular flowchart series: **"Am I acting like a fucking adult?"** which encompasses all of our FUNdamentals (and then some).

Stick with me, kid, and oh, the places we'll go!

The evolution of a Total Fucking Grownup

If you know me, you know I love to establish parameters. LOVE IT. So to kick off part I, here's the spectrum of adulting that I'll be referencing throughout the book, so you can take a look at where you stand — and where you want to end up.

Now let's meet each of our players:

Actual Babies

By virtue of being as far from full-grown as it gets, Actual Babies are the definition of immature. And they don't come into this world knowing how to be responsible or accountable, either. They don't even know how their toes work! But over time, babies learn. They grow into their human brains and bodies, and eventually get to a stage where immaturity is no longer an inherent condition; it's just a poor excuse for bad behavior. And then they're old enough to be able to seek out the tools they need to act responsibly and be accountable *for* their actions—at which point, they can go one of three ways…

Big Fucking Babies (BFBs)

These are the adults-in-age-only who've had plenty of time and opportunity to grow the fuck up, but won't make the effort. Like Actual Babies, they are lazy and needy and unreliable and inconsiderate, but unlike their infant counterparts, they have no excuse. And it's really no way to live. Like, yes, they do whatever they want all day with no regard for how it affects other people — which may seem freeing — but eventually those other people will stop being friends with them, doing business with them, and putting up with their bullshit. I'm lookin' at you, James Corden.

(Oh, and people will also use anonymous surveys to gleefully report on BFBs' egregious actions and behavior. More on that in a sec.)

Theoretical Adults

They're old enough and knowledgeable enough and experienced enough to act maturely and responsibly — and they want to! — but for any number of reasons, they're having a hard time putting it all together. They're not lazy, but maybe they're disorganized or easily overwhelmed. They might be more than alright at being polite, but haven't yet cracked the code of self-sufficiency (or vice versa). Or they're good at holding themselves accountable and apologizing for their mistakes — but clearly not so good at *learning* from those mistakes, or they wouldn't keep making them, eh?

> I'm guessing "Theoretical Adult" is where you're hanging out, since Actual Babies can't read this book, Big Fucking Babies wouldn't care to read it, and Total Fucking Grownups don't need it.

Total Fucking Grownups (TFGs)

Like the moniker suggests, TFGs are the full package. They're mature and responsible, capable and resourceful, self-sufficient and successful, trusted and respected. They know how to take accountability and learn from their mistakes (which they make fewer and fewer of, natch). They work a little harder, a LOT smarter, and they get *all* the perks.

They've got the tools and they know how to use 'em — for their own and everyone else's benefit.

PRO-DULT TIP: You know what Total Fucking Grownups *don't* have? Dishes and coffee cups and mirrors and other possessions coated in gummy price tag residue, which, no matter how many times you try, is not going to come off in the dishwasher. A few swipes with a cotton ball covered in the magical elixir known as Goo Gone will erase it. (Also useful on scissors that are covered in pine sap after you used them to snip unruly branches off your Christmas tree. And on your hands, which are very sticky.) Honestly, if my publisher hasn't figured out a way to bundle this book at Target with a bottle of that sweet GG, I may need to speak to the sales director.

Okay, so now back to my survey, and the question that turned out to be the most revealing of them all:

Imagine an adult you know who acts like a Big Fucking Baby. What makes you think that about them?

I admit I phrased this Q in a very intentional way — because if there's one thing I've learned from administering a bunch of these things, it's that not all of us are self-aware enough to identify our own shortcomings (nor candid enough to admit to them), but that *everybody* goes no-holds-barred on *other people* in an anonymous Google Form.

And THAT'S when you get the goods.

Here are the qualities that rose to the top (er, sank to the bottom?) when it came to being branded a BFB:

BIG FUCKING BABIES

Rude/disrespectful	Unreliable
Ungrateful	Never take initiative
Complain all the time	Let others clean up their mess
Never apologize	Lazy
Act entitled/spoiled	Always making excuses
Have no self-control	Won't take accountability

Now, I want you to take a good, long look at that list. **See any-thing you recognize?** I have a hunch that you do — even if it's just a brief, uncomfortable pang when you cast your eyes over the word "unreliable." Because if there's anything else I've learned from all my survey-taking and advice-giving, it's that all of the shit *other* people do that rubs us the wrong way and sends us cattily tap-tap-tapping away in one of Auntie Sarah's questionnaires?

We're doing it too.

At least some of it, sometimes. I mean, why else would you be here if you didn't know, deep down, that you need help? It's okay. There's no shame in that game. A certain anti-guru, for example, has not always been so great at admitting fault.* It's taken years of self-reflection and effort to get to a place where I can suck it up, cop to a mistake, apologize if necessary, and move on without getting all bent out of shape over it.†

(I can help you get there too, in part IV. Watch this space.)

Anyway, what I'm saying is, each and every well-intentioned one of us is bound to have a few entries in the Big Fucking Baby col-umns, whether we're ready to admit it or not. The important thing is that by the end of the book, you have all the skills you could pos-sibly need to rep Total Fucking Grownup, 24/7:

---

* Mostly because I'm almost always right.
† On the rare occasion when I am to blame.

TOTAL FUCKING GROWNUPS

Polite/respectful	Reliable
Show gratitude	Independent
Not whiny little bitches	Considerate
Admit fault	Resourceful/proactive
Don't take people/things for granted	Accept criticism
Emotionally stable	Fix mistakes and learn from them

Now check out *that* list. **I bet you recognize yourself in some of these qualities too, and good for you!** We all contain multitudes. But do Auntie Sarah a favor — if you get to, say, the section on being considerate, or the chapter on being resourceful, and you think *I don't need this, I've got it covered,* and you're tempted to skip ahead?

Don't.

It's all connected, friend-o. I didn't weave a complex tapestry of adult wisdom **into a fun, practical, easy-to-use baller manual of life advice** for you to treat it like an à la carte menu at Chipotle.

Okay, so now that you know what being a Total Fucking Grownup looks like, you may wonder why, exactly, **you ought to want to make the effort to become one.** After all, any Theoretical Adult can watch all the garbage TV their heart desires and eat ice

cream for dinner — both of which are undeniably attractive prop-
ositions and easy enough to implement when you're the one who's
[finally!] in charge.

Fair point.

But I guarantee that a full-fledged, fully realized TFG is destined for bigger wins than Bravo marathons or Chubby Hubby on
demand, so let's **dial up the GTFU MO-tivation and talk about
what's in it for YOU, shall we?**

Finish your chores and you can go play

When we were kids, most of us had to clear the table or fold the
laundry before we were allowed to go off and do the fun stuff. And
it turns out that adulting is much the same, except that we're facing
bigger tasks and greater challenges, and the fruits of those labors
are *also* bigger and better than heading off to a sleepover or being
let loose on the playground for a half-hour freedom run.

Like, sure, you have to pay rent — but you also get to hang a
disco ball in your bathroom if you feel like it. Disco showers,
FTW! And yeah, if you want to get your whole security deposit
back, you're going to have to fill in the screw holes when you give
up your lease ... which is where a Theoretical Adult might just

say "Eh, fuck it" and take the hit. Whereas a TFG would plaster responsibly, receive full recompense from their landlord, pay their movers, *and* have enough left over to purchase a dedicated Chubby Hubby freezer for their new apartment.

This, friends. This is #GOALS.

And those are just the tip of the perkberg. There's quite a lot of GTFU MO-tivation packed into these pages, much of it in the form of **straight-up REWARDS.**

For example, in addition to mandating that you finish your chores, your parents probably also told you more than once to **"Mind your manners."** And good for them! They wanted to raise you right, and also minimize the number of dirty looks they'd get from fellow patrons when they toted you along to Applebee's for Double Crunch Shrimp Night.

But guess what? Being polite, personable, and respectful will get you much *more* in your adult life than merely the cocktail sauce passed at dinner and/or not being asked to leave before dessert. **Tell me: Do you like promotions and raises at work and free drinks at restaurants and upgrades at hotels and functional relationships with your friends and family?**

Then it is your lucky motherfucking day! In part II, I'll lay down deets on these and more big, beautiful bonuses of being on your best behavior.

Or how about when the 'rents pestered you nightly to **"Do your homework."** They weren't sadists; they just wanted you to pass into a new grade year after year so you could graduate with the skills to get a job and move out of their house. Totally reasonable.

But now that you're an adult, the concept of "doing your homework" is more expansive — it involves researching your options; weighing risks, benefits, and consequences; and coming prepared — and there's a lot more to gain than a B+ in algebra (or even a job and a place of your own). **Doing your due diligence helps you plan kick-ass vacations, score hard-to-get reservations at the hottest place in town, and even get a great deal on a new dishwasher.** Trust me, adults get excited about that last one.

We'll dive into those rewards and more in part III.

Oh, and how about the all-time classic, **"Go clean your room."** While I'm sure Mom/Dad/Grandma have been known to wax rhapsodic about your younger years — when you were super-adorable but they also had to run around picking up all the crap you left in your wake because you didn't know where anything went — I'd also bet my left ovary that they were quite eager to turn cleanup duty over to you at the earliest convenience. By the time middle school rolled around, it may have felt like they were just using you for free labor (which, maybe).

But hear me out, because knowing how to clean up after yourself ALSO makes you the kind of adult whose friends will invite you to join them at a swanky Airbnb vacation villa because you can be trusted not to leave it looking like *Jackass* 7 just wrapped. Not bad. Plus, there's even more to be gained from knowing how to clean up your *figurative* messes — aka owning up to your mistakes and stepping up to fix them.

We'll get to all of the above in part IV.

PRO-DULT TIP: Is it a coincidence that the words A-D-U-L-T and A-P-R-O-N both have five letters? Maybe! Should you take it as a sign from the universe that it's worth it to invest in a cooking coverup that will save one or more of your favorite shirts from future ruin? Definitely!

And finally, as if all the **REWARDS** weren't enough, there's the other equally valuable side to our GTFU MO-tivational coin: **RELIEF.**

I won't lie. Along with the fun stuff, adulthood comes with its share of tight deadlines, important meetings, painful break-ups, prickly family dynamics, and then some. And no matter how maturely, responsibly, and accountably you handle such grownup challenges, they don't tend to end in disco showers and dessert-on-demand.

But let me tell you: **that sweet, sweet relief can be just as precious.**

The relief, for example, of feeling confident and capable going into a difficult situation, because you've *prepared* for this; instead of sweating bullets and getting a workout just from trying to cover your ass.

The relief of knowing that no matter what happens, you did the best you could.

The relief of having dispensed with an annoying thing, so it can't annoy you any further.

The relief of putting your emotions out there — even if it was scary — so you don't have to deal with them alone anymore.

And there you have it, all the GTFU MO-tivation you could ever need to go out there and do this adult thing. **REWARD and RELIEF, "R&R."** That's the grownup version of "and then you can go play," and it is wicked fucking worth it.

So with our parameters established and our #GOALS in mind, it's time for the real work to begin. But don't be nervous! **The first step toward becoming a Total Fucking Grownup is as easy**

as learning your ABCs. It's just a slightly different version than you're used to…

A is for *Action*

B is for *Behavior*

C is for *Consequences*

In other words: your ACTIONS and BEHAVIOR have CONSEQUENCES.

Learn it, live it.

You know better than that

With regard to consequences, Actual Babies get a pass. They're not expected to know any better. They are expected to poop their diapers and scream their resultant displeasure, and, despite those prevailing characteristics, people still cater to their every whim and take pictures of them with marinara sauce all over their faces and inexplicably deem it "adorable."

Ideally the adults in the room are modeling best practices, and eventually — from our toddler to teen years — we're meant to start mimicking them. Then, as adults in our own right, we ARE expected to know full well that indiscriminate pooping and screaming is not cool, and we SHOULD be thoroughly unsurprised if we risk indulging in it anyway and find ourselves escorted out of Whole Foods in handcuffs.

Come on, pal. You know better than that.

Understanding **what consequences are and how they work** is a key component of growing the fuck up, and one with which you're undoubtedly already familiar. Think back to punishments the authority figures in your life may have leveled for messing up or behaving like a brat. Those were "bad consequences."

Did you enjoy them? I didn't think so.

Did you know they were going to happen when you decided to act/behave like you did? I'm guessing you did, kid.

And yet — AND YET — **plenty of Theoretical Adults still do not always** *apply* **what they definitely** *already know* **about consequences nearly enough in their day-to-day.** Instead, they A & B with no thought to the potential Cs, and do stupid shit like blowing deadline after deadline and finding themselves on the ass end of an HR exit interview before they can say, "Wait! Can I get a do-over?"

Dude, you are so fired.

Total Fucking Grownups, however, understand that **bad**

consequences don't just *happen* — they're *brought on* by your actions and behavior.

You miss curfew; you get grounded.

You get a D in math; they take away your phone.

You sass your mother; all of the above.

By the same token, **your GOOD actions and behavior can bring GOOD consequences,** aka outcomes of the reward and relief variety.

You bring the car back unscathed; you get to use it again.

You study hard for a test; you get an A.

You're always nice to the neighbor kid; they let you jump on their trampoline.

Pretty straightforward, right? And as we know from the third branch of our GTFU MO, **adults hold themselves *accountable* for their actions and behavior** — so why not **make it EASIER and MORE PLEASANT on yourself** by tipping the consequences in your favor on the front end?

In order to jump-start your trajectory into TFG territory (and yes, that was a trampoline pun), here's a nifty two-step method for conquering the concept of consequences, once and for all.

ANTICIPATE & ORCHESTRATE

1. **ANTICIPATE the consequences.**
   Ask yourself: *What happens if [I act like X/behave like Y]?*

2. **ORCHESTRATE the outcome,** whether that means *avoiding* bad consequences (e.g., RELIEF) or *inviting* good ones (e.g., REWARD).

   Ask yourself: *What can I do to get the best possible result here?*

Then act/behave accordingly. That's it!

Ready for some examples? Cool. **We'll start with "avoiding bad consequences."**

Say you've got a final exam on Monday. You don't feel like studying for it this weekend, and you're tempted to fake a family emergency to get out of having to take it. Let's anticipate the consequences of this action. (There can be multiple iterations here; don't be shy.)

What happens if I lie to get out of studying for/taking this test?

Maybe you'll get away with the fake-out, but you'll still have to take a makeup exam and, ergo, still eventually have to study for it, ruining a future weekend anyway. Or maybe you'll get caught in the lie, get disciplined for it, AND still have to study for/take a makeup exam. Oof.

These are all objectively likely consequences, none of which result in a great outcome for you. Good thing you have the power to **orchestrate** a better one...

What can I do to get the best result?

Given the details, I don't see much room for pure, unadulterated "reward" here. But if you behave like a mature, responsible adult who doesn't lie about Grandma's heart condition, buckle down with the books now, and just take the damn test on Monday, at least you're not digging yourself an even deeper hole that'll take even *more* time and energy to climb out of later, and that's a relief!

If you think this was an overly simplistic scenario with an obvious answer, then I refer you back to "plenty of Theoretical Adults still do not always apply what they definitely already know about consequences." My whole *raison d'être* is to simplify this shit for you, so you CAN and WILL remember it. Two steps. One life-changing concept. You're welcome.

Now let's look at a situation where Anticipate & Orchestrate could help you not only *avoid* the worst (RELIEF), but potentially *enjoy* the best (REWARD).

Say you're in the midst of your first (or, hell, your seventeenth) apartment search, and you've finally found a place you love with roommates who seem cool. They want you to come back for a coffee and chat before they decide who gets to move in, but they've scheduled it for a day you're supposed to be filling in at the animal shelter, and it'll be tough to get to the meet-up on time. What's your strategy?

Remember: your actions and behavior have consequences. **Anticipate, orchestrate!**

What happens if I try to squeeze both in, and I'm late to the interview?

Maaaaaaaybe it won't make a difference, but your future roomies wouldn't be wrong to assume "not on time" equals "not that interested" or worse, "probably late on rent checks too." If there's competition for this spot, you're not doing yourself any favors by showing up past due. Especially if you arrive covered in parakeet poop.

What can I do to get the best result here?

You could request a later start time, and again, maaaaaaaybe that would be fine. The group might even be impressed that you're the kind of person who does volunteer work. But you also risk annoying or making things difficult on *them,* which doesn't seem like the ideal strategy, especially if you have other options.

Given the stakes, it seems like begging off or trading your volunteer shift would be the safer bet. I mean, a) it's a *volunteer* shift and b) I'm guessing the *shelter* folks would understand how important it is that you secure a roof over your head. And if you arrive at the apartment bearing a box of cookies, a bunch of flowers, and/or a few well-rehearsed, thoughtful reasons why you think you'd fit in so well here, that'll probably improve your chances.*

That wasn't too taxing, was it? There's no reason in the world that you can't go out there and **use everything you *already know* about consequences to guide your actions and behavior toward the most desirable outcome.**

---

* Heads up: part II contains a lot more re: well-mannered strategery, a TFG specialty.

BFBs to the left of you, TFGs to the right. You know which way to go.

The C-Cycle

Further in our study of the FUNdamentals, I want to introduce three skill sets that separate the teeny-tiny hoomans who *can't* live on their own (Actual Babies) and the adults who *could* but refuse to try (Big Fucking Babies) from those who may be trying but not yet doing it particularly *well* (Theoretical Adults), and then the adultiest of them all, the Total Fucking Grownups. These skills are:

CRITICAL THINKING

COMMUNICATION

COPING

We'll start with a primer on each of them, and then look at how they operate together, in action.

Critical thinking

Actual Babies have virtually no life experience. Kids have a little. But you? You have a medium-to-fuck-ton, and as luck would have it, every

<table>
<tr><td>

**You'll use critical
thinking to**

Identify and weigh
consequences
Strategize for best
outcomes
Learn from the past and
apply toward the future

</td></tr>
</table>

past experience under your belt provides a valuable data point. Critical thinking is the process of sifting through all of that accumulated information — all those consequences, all those outcomes — and using it to help make better decisions in the *future*. **The benefit of hindsight is increased foresight.**

Now, under the auspices of critical thinking, let's look at a super adult-y pursuit — the job interview — and compare the BFB-to-TFG approach, with a Theoretical Adult thrown in for control.

BFBs practice zero-to-minimal preparation. Lord knows how they scored an interview in the first place. Family connections? In any case, they have not thought critically about any of this — appropriate interview attire; how long it'll take to get there, and whether additional time should be built in for potential public transportation snafus; with whom they'll be meeting (Is it HR, or the CEO? Who cares? Surprises are fun!); or what they should be trying to get across about their experience and enthusiasm to maximize their chances of being hired. They've learned nothing from their past few #interviewfails, and because they also haven't thought through the consequences of *not* getting the job, they're about to face the unenviable prospect of having to choose between being able to pay rent or having to sleep on Todd's couch for a few months, and they're not prepared for that, either. (Alas, neither is Todd.)

Theoretical Adults understand that it's important to show up on time and have padded their commute by an extra fifteen minutes just in case; but they forgot to check their good interview outfit for stains and wrinkles, so there's that. They've probably researched their potential employer, but maybe stopped short of rehearsing any talking points. Will any of those hiccups hinder their chances of getting hired? Maybe, maybe not. But why take the chance? Todd's couch is lumpy, and did I mention his dog sheds like a motherfucker?

TFGs will arrive promptly and well pressed, armed with an extra paper copy of their résumé, just in case. They've done their due diligence on the company and maybe even talked to someone they know who works there to get an inside track on hiring practices. They've given some thought to what happens if they get the job (i.e., what to do if the offer is subpar and they need to negotiate; how much notice to give at their current job; and how much blessed vacation time to build in between), and also if they *don't* get it — and they're prepared for either outcome.

Bottom line: When it comes to flexing those critical thinking skills, you do neither yourself nor Todd any favors by faking and mistaking your way through life. And unlike a teeny-tiny infant hooman, you have access to all the information you need, the free will to seek it out, and the brainpower to process it to your advantage. Use it.

Communication

Actual Babies can't really communicate. You can, and that's half the battle — which is great, because unfortunately you cannot order takeout by babbling nonsense into the phone or ask for time off by squawking in your boss's general direction. You've got to be able to *assess* your own needs ('Sup, critical thinking!) and also *express* them effectively to other people in order to get what you want in life. Learning how to string together words to create meaning — and then honing those words to a fine, effective, and persuasive point — is where it's AT.

We'll get down and dirty in all kinds of communication tactics as we go along, but for now, let's stick with our job interview example and look at how our candidates stack up when it's time to use their words:

BFBs, as mentioned, have not spent any time thinking about what they want to say or how to say it. They definitely have not perused the company website to get a sense of the tone and lingo of their prospective employer. They're destined to say "like" and "um" a few billion times, and when the interview concludes with "Do you have any questions for us?" the best they can do is "Where is the bathroom? I have to go before I get back on the train, thanks!"

Theoretical Adults know enough to be polite and attentive, and they think/hope that'll disguise their lack of hard-core prep. But while the words that come out of their mouths will be well-mannered, they may also be somewhat wishy-washy, costing them an opportunity to make a good impression *and* a personal connection with their audience. (Whereas if they'd spent a little time doing social media recon, they might have discovered that their interviewer is a fellow Red Sox fan, a nugget they could have used to craft a memorable bit o' small talk.) With half an hour to make their case, the odds are not exactly in their favor. Many will fake it; a few might make it.

TFGs show up ready to shoot their shot. They've thought about what makes them the best candidate for the job and they've practiced expressing that info politely, concisely, and persuasively. They also remember what happened the first time they were up for a job and got blindsided with the "Tell us your greatest weakness" question, so they've prepared a well-thought-out reply for that one, if needed. (And this time it won't be "I sometimes clash with authority figures." Oops.)

Bottom line: If you're reading this book, then you already possess the basic comprehension/communication skills you'll need for our upcoming adventures in TFG-ing. Like I said, half the battle, already fought. I'll help you level up, so you can consistently come out on top.

PRO-DULT TIP: Perhaps this is a generational thing for those of us who came of age when email was all shiny and new, but if you started out with an address like Trip4Balls@AOL.com *and you still use it to this day,* I hate to rain on your self-expression parade, but it's high time to retire that shit. The same goes for more modern electronic monikers, such as TikTok handles and YouTube channels. I looked at a lot of résumés back in my hiring days and you know who doesn't get a callback? "WorkBitchBritney" and "SoccerDude69."

Coping

In an analogy that I will continue flogging for the remainder of this book, let us consider the plight of an Actual Baby who a) may or may not know what they want, b) can't express it or pursue it even if they do know, and c) has no way of processing/dealing with *not* getting it.

Uh-oh, I smell a tantrum coming on...

Cathartic? Perhaps. But while lying on your back in a crib screaming until you're red in the face may seem like an attractive option every now and then, it is not a recommended lifelong go-to coping mechanism. Nor, for that matter, is whining, pouting, or refusing to come out of your room until the end of days.

Life does not always turn out how you want it to. And if you care to power through the tough spots with minimal damage to

> **You'll use coping to**
>
> Handle difficult emotions
> Push through
>   disappointment
> Bounce back from failure

your relationships, reputation, and mental health, you'll need to be able to cope effectively — both inwardly (e.g., taking criticism and accepting accountability for your own role in whatever failure or disappointment has befallen you) and outwardly (e.g., not going apeshit on anyone else who may be responsible for those failures/disappointments).

We'll get to all of that in detail in due time, but for now let's take one last look at our interview and its aftermath:

BFBs did not get the job, shocking no one but themselves. They were prepared neither for the interview, nor for what would happen when they blew the interview, which means they are simultaneously disappointed, pissed off, freaked out, possibly throwing a real, live tantrum, and wasting valuable time and energy on all those unhelpful states of being when they really ought to be accepting their fate, learning from their myriad mistakes, and getting back out there with a nifty two-step method for anticipating consequences and orchestrating a better outcome next time around.

Theoretical Adults may have squeaked by and gotten the gig. (I know this because I've worked with plenty of them in my time.)

So that's settled, and hey, congrats where congrats are due! But with new employment will come new responsibilities, new systems, new bosses and colleagues, and plenty of new tests of one's critical thinking and communication skills, which may not always work out for the fake-it-till-you-make-it crowd. If and when those skills *do* fall short, the ability to cope with the fallout will come in mighty handy. Keep reading, is what I'm saying.

TFGs probably got the offer and maybe even negotiated a higher starting salary while they were at it. Woot! But if they didn't? They regroup and revisit the game plan they'd already made to deal with this potential outcome. Perhaps they dash off a polite email to the HR rep asking if there was anything they could have done better to make the cut. (They do *not* dash off an embittered IG Story and tag their would-be employer.) The situation is not awesome, but they're handling it, because that's what adults *do*.

Bottom line: Suck it up, Buttercup.

In most scenarios that life throws your way, you'll need to engage in **CRITICAL THINKING** — first to identify what you want and need, and then to anticipate the **CONSEQUENCES** of your actions and behavior before you attempt to **COMMUNICATE** those wants/needs to others. And whatever the outcome, you'll have to **COPE** with the **CONSEQUENCES** on your own as well as **COMMUNICATE** any (potential) disappointment to others, and engage in another round of **CRITICAL THINKING** about where to go from there.

That right there is a ride on the C-Cycle. It's no Space Mountain, but I do what I can.

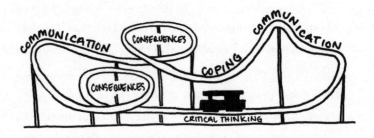

The extent to which you're able to hang on to this ride without anxiety-puking or shutting your eyes the whole time and silently begging for death is directly proportionate to your evolution as a TFG — and in parts II, III, and IV, I'll walk you through all kinds of ways to grease those adulting gears and make the whole experience as smooth as possible.

So, what do you say? Ready to give adulting a whirl?

NOOOO! I DON'T *WANNA!*

Ah, yes. Well, I can't say I didn't *anticipate* a little resistance right about now. And I feel ya, I really do, says the adult woman currently juggling a book deadline, hurricane cleanup, Covid recovery, and a fucking termite infestation because OF COURSE.

As one of my survey takers put it, being an adult often entails **"sucking it up and doing things even when they're hard."** So true. While we're at it, let's add **"doing things you don't want to do because they are really fucking annoying."**

Still, as the reigning adultiest adult in the room, it's my duty to remind you that **in order to get all of the perks that come with being a Total Fucking Grownup, you have to deal with the less perky parts too.** To live on your own in a sweet party pad, you must pay rent on said sweet pad. To unlock the mysteries and unearth the treasures of functional adulthood, you must power through the rest of the book.

Chores first, then you can go play. That's just how it is.

And while I'm no fairy god-auntie who can wave a magic wand and disappear your rent bill or effortlessly download all of this life-changing content directly to your brain, I did promise you "easier" and "more pleasant" and that I shall provide. As such, and to round out part I, it's my pleasure to present you with two widely applicable tricks for **developing a better APPROACH and ATTITUDE to the stuff you don't *wanna* but still *hafta* do.**

Enter: **HABITS** and **INCENTIVES.**

Brush your teeth

Habits (the good kind) are a cool tool for more than just fighting plaque and kicking cavities to the curb. Turning off the lights whenever you leave the room, for example. This may have been a habit some of our fathers somewhat aggressively instilled in us as kids ("What do you think this is, a lighthouse for the blind?"), but in their defense, it does lead to lower energy costs — and when you're the one paying, you'll appreciate Dad's intensity on the subject. Cutting the lights when you're not using them is a much less painful way to achieve "manageable electric bill" than, say, having to live in the dark for six days at the end of the month to make up for your earlier high-wattage profligacy.

> ### Habits (the bad kind)
>
> Biting your nails
> Smoking cigarettes
> Leaving your keys in the door
> Leaving pee on the seat

Other ways you can employ good habits to help you more **EASILY** and **PLEASANTLY** achieve your ideal adult form include:

Check your bank balance daily; avoid accidental overdrafts.

Dust your apartment once a week; your asthmatic Tinder date might just spend the night next time.

And don't get me started on monthly breast self-exams. A habit that could save your life? SIGN ME UP.

Daily, weekly, monthly — whatever — **there is enormous value in getting into a groove.** And sure, you have to put in the work to initiate the habit (more on that in a sec), but once you do that? Man, you are *golden.* Instead of having to dread and/or scramble to deal with those difficult and/or annoying adult tasks, **habits help you:**

Optimize
You have so much to think and worry about and deal with on any given day; wouldn't it be nice to put some of it on autopilot?

For example, if I am to have any hope of muddling through my morning, I require caffeine immediately upon waking. And you know what I NEVER feel like doing as soon as

I wake up? Making coffee! So in my household, we have a habit of prepping the coffeemaker the night before, which means that instead of spilling coffee grounds all over the counter because I'm still half asleep and then having to clean them up without the benefit of caffeine in my system — all I have to do is push a button and wait five minutes. #Blessed

(For the fancy pants among us, I hear they also make coffee machines with built-in timers that you can set the night before. What a time to be alive!)

Solve for X

If you're always running late to classes/meetings/lunch dates (or forgetting about them entirely), make it a habit to set your calendar reminder to "15 minutes before," for that extra kick in the caboose.

And if you have an unusually early a.m. appointment, you can do what I do and set the calendar notification to "18 hours before" so you remember to set your wake-up alarm in the first place... and then set another alarm just in case. What? You know how I am in the morning.

Building this kind of step into your prep is a lot *easier* and *more pleasant* than having to sheepishly beg for other people's notes on what you missed, or getting reamed out by your professor/boss/BFFs on the regular. As is, say, making it a habit to check the booth/car/taxi/bus seat/stadium bleachers for your phone and wallet *before* you get up or get out, in order to eliminate both the pesky tendency you have to lose your stuff and the resulting pesky items added to your to-do list: "buy new phone and cancel all my cards."

Make sucky things suck less

Turning a less-than-awesome task into a habit can make it easier and more pleasant each time you do it — even if that means doing it a bit more often and when you don't particularly feel like it — instead of *supermotherfuckingdifficultandannoying* EVERY time...when you ALSO won't particularly feel like it!

For example, taking out the trash whenever it's pretty full, not waiting until an old chicken carcass has reanimated to beg you to put it out of its stinky misery. Or in my case, spending five minutes sweeping my terrace every morning while I wait for the coffee to brew, which is vastly preferable to getting down on my hands and knees with bleach and a rough sponge once a month because I foolishly gave the frog poop time to adhere to the cement and OMG WHAT IS THAT STUFF MADE OF?!?*

Habits: low-impact hacks to amortize adulting over time. You gotta love 'em.

PRO-DULT TIP: Speaking of adulting hacks, I was well into my forties before I learned that there's a little arrow on your fuel gauge that indicates which side your gas tank is on. Exceedingly useful when driving a rental or otherwise unfamiliar car, or just for those of us who are easily confused by concepts like "right" and "left."

If any of this is starting to sound depressing, note that **habits can also be used to engender good stuff, not just streamline the hard/annoying stuff.**

Like, it's one thing to harness the power of habits to keep your kitchen trash from going nuclear, or to keep your electric bill in check, but **being disciplined about making small sacrifices**

---

* Caribbean life is lovely in many ways, but frog poop is the bane of my existence.

now for big rewards later can ALSO, for example, send you on bougie vacations with perfect skin and a decent understanding of the local wine lists. To wit:

Saving a little bit of money every week for a year will ensure you have enough to go to Ibiza for Christmas instead of just hoping there'll be a great deal on last-minute flights. (And being extremely bummed if there isn't.)

Making it a habit to apply zit cream every night before bed even if you don't currently have any zits can help prevent you from *getting* zits at a really inopportune time, such as the day before you're leaving for Spain.

Reading four pages a day of *Decoding Spanish Wine: A Beginner's Guide to the High Value, World Class Wines of Spain* for the month leading up to your trip will help you get more bang for your drinks budget, and maybe impress a hunky waiter while you're at it. Talk about GTFU MO-tivation. Yum.

Finally, beyond making your life easier and more pleasant, **developing good habits will lead to *others viewing you* as a more reliable, put-together, forward-thinking individual.**
WHICH WILL ALSO MAKE YOUR LIFE EASIER AND

MORE PLEASANT. How? Because when you're calmly and happily doing your adult thang, people will notice the results. They'll see, for example, that you're keen to set goals and follow through, and they'll respect and trust you instead of yelling at you to show up on time and take your own goddamn notes.

Act like an adult *and* get treated like one! It's right there in the subtitle, folks.

Okeydokey. So, this is the point in my draft manuscript where my editor would write in the margin **"All helpful, but how do you *form* a habit?"** and I would spend five minutes being all "Duh, you just do it!" before remembering that this stuff isn't so obvious for everybody and that if I didn't come here to drop very fucking explicit instructions, what kind of anti-guru would I be?

HOW TO FORM A HABIT IN 3 EASY STEPS

STEP 1:
IDENTIFY (the need).

STEP 2:
IMPLEMENT (a solution).

STEP 3:
REPEAT STEP 2 until you no longer think of it as "STEP 2" but rather just "A THING I DO."

For example, are you always losing your keys? Need = identified!

What would be a good solution? How about "Always put them away in the same place when you come home, keep them in the same pocket of your pants or bag when you go out, and for the love of God check for them *before* you get out of the taxi?"

Great! Now commit to implementing those solutions Every. Damn. Time. **Repetition is how you turn a discrete action into a habit.** And it's also how you get the most value out of all the time you spent identifying problems and coming *up* with solutions. Once you turn step 2 into just a thing you do, you no longer have to think much about it at all, do ya?

PRO-DULT TIP: "You can do anything for six months." This mantra, or a variation on it — i.e., "two weeks" or "a year" — is something I tell myself whenever I'm facing an onerous task or unpleasant situation, like embarking on Invisalign or waiting an extra year to quit my job so my 401k would be fully vested. (Or, say, making it through yet another day of a seemingly endless pandemic-era lockdown…) Experts disagree on how long it takes to form a habit — anywhere from twenty-one days to two months to nearly a year, on average. And while any/all of those figures may seem daunting, just think about all the other stuff you've done (or perhaps "endured") in service to a greater goal? If you want this, you've got this. You can do anything for six months.

Remember: **Optimize, solve for X, and make sucky things suck less.** In your quest to become a certified TFG, forming some choice habits will take you far. And when you need an extra dose of GTFU MO-tivation, my next tip is yours for the taking.

Here, have a lollipop!

When it comes to the hardest/most annoying parts of adulting, sometimes — and much like the stale lollipops my childhood dentist doled out after a cleaning — the baked-in rewards aren't that great.

Unfortunately, there may not be much relief, either. When doing your taxes, for example. While I suppose "not getting arrested by the federal government" is, in some sense, a "relief," tax prep is so tedious (even if you hire somebody to help you with it), and expensive (*especially* if you hire somebody to help you with it), that even I, a Total Fucking Grownup, have occasionally wondered whether it would be easier and more pleasant to go on the lam in a country without an extradition treaty than to continue saving all of my fucking receipts and plugging them into a fucking Excel spreadsheet every year until I die.*

---

* To be clear, I accept the grownup responsibility of *paying* taxes; I just hatehate-hate *doing them.*

Anyway, this is where **INCENTIVES** come in handy — by which I mean **self-determined bonuses that motivate you** to get shit done *and* offer you something for your trouble that isn't a stupid lemon Blow Pop or your annual reprieve from being taken to tax court.

When the hardest/most annoying adulting comes calling and motivation is scarce, **Auntie Sarah says: treat yo'*self*.** (Or rather, PLAN to treat yo'self. If you take your reward first, that's not incentivizing; that's cheating.)

For example, these days if I'm going to submit to a semiannual scraping of my tender middle-aged gums, I prefer to know there'll be a stiff martini waiting for me to suck on after the fact. Mmmm. So cold, so soothing.

Other ideas for **incentivizing yourself to get out there and do the adult thing** include:

Upgrading to that cool slim wallet you've been eyeing, after you successfully survive going to the DMV to renew your license

Planning a special dinner out for after you complete your colonoscopy (and after you're allowed to eat solid foods again)

Grabbing a back massage after you've hefted the last pile of books into those moving boxes

Inexpensive
rewards for an adult
job well done

Turn off notifications for
the rest of the weekend
Binge your favorite show
Go to the park
Find a puppy to play with
Wax the you-know-what
and call you-know-who

And note: incentives don't have to cost a lot of money — or any at all. There are oodles of affordable ways to turn "I don't wanna!" into "Actually, that wasn't so bad." They can be physically or emotionally satisfying, or psychologically soothing. Point of fact: I incentivized myself to finish writing this chapter by promising myself a much-needed walk on the beach, which was all three. (Okay, I also had a martini.)

Got it?

Excellent, I knew you were going to be a quick study!

So now, for your first exercise in pro-dulting — which is to say, in **making things EASIER and MORE PLEASANT for yourself** — I want you to think about ways that you could start employing my first two GTFU tips.

Like, today.

DIFFICULT OR ANNOYING SHIT I HAVE
TO DEAL WITH

_____   _____
_____   _____
_____   _____
_____   _____
_____   _____
_____   _____
_____   _____
_____   _____

HABITS THAT WOULD   ## INCENTIVES THAT WOULD
MAKE IT EASIER   ## MAKE IT MORE PLEASANT

_____   _____
_____   _____
_____   _____
_____   _____
_____   _____
_____   _____
_____   _____

BOOM. Just like that, you're cruising toward TFG territory with an attitude-and-approach adjustment that could make all the difference, if you commit to it. How does it feel?

Would you say you're, perhaps, a little more *confident* that you can do this thing?

Secret Bonus C: Confidence

Many of my survey responders reported that they struggle with confidence — a quality that, ironically, I think we're more likely *born with,* rather than one we have to develop proactively, such as "being organized."

I mean, babies can't make it to a meeting on time, but they have no problem hogging the limelight, do they? And every four-year-old I've ever known would declare themselves a "BEAUTIFUL AWESOME UNICORN" in a heartbeat, whereas many, many teens and adults have seen that innate confidence slowly wrung from their prefrontal cortexes as their brains developed to process feelings of failure and emotions like shame and embarrassment.

Fun times!

If you, too, struggle with this stuff, the good news is that there are plenty of books out there that are entirely devoted to helping you boost confidence and build self-esteem, from the inside out.

(I know this in part because I wrote one myself called *You Do You,* and it's a banger.) *Grow the Fuck Up* does not retread all of that territory, but it will have some similar effects — except this time, working on you from the outside in.

If you make the effort to approach life in a mature, responsible way, you'll succeed more often than you fail.

Each of those successes — as well as the failures you've learned to hold yourself accountable for and to cope with so impressively, adult-ily well — continually reinforce the idea that you have really, truly got this. All of *that,* along with the admiration and appreciation of others who will take notice of and applaud your various victory laps, is bound to give you a heaping helping of the confidence you seek.

It's yet another C for the Cycle. Hands in the air, wind on your face, yelling at the top of your lungs. In a good way.

My hope is that everything you learn from this book about becoming an adult will *also* **help you recapture the confidence of a carefree kid** who hasn't yet been given any reason to feel that they are anything less than a beautiful, awesome unicorn. We'll get there in part by building the mental muscles like self-awareness and self-control that enable you to **TFG your way through life AND hold your head up high.**

Which, I gotta say, even shameless little babies can't do that. (Weak necks.)

* * *

And that'll do it for part I! Fairly easy and pleasant, was it not? You've laid a solid foundation for your adult endeavors — summoned some quality GTFUMO-tivation; memorized your ABCs; learned to anticipate and orchestrate consequences; gotten a taste of critical thinking, communication, and coping, with the lure of building confidence along the way; and dabbled in two supremely practical strategies for tackling the hardest, most annoying shit adulting has to offer.

Now it's time to focus on the finer points.

The next three parts of the book explore **MATURITY, RESPONSIBILITY,** and **ACCOUNTABILITY.** And I swear on the life of Robert Ray Knight that it'll be entertaining, but if at any point you start to feel overwhelmed, you can always sneak a look at my handy-dandy flowchart to help you get back on track.

Think of it like a preapproved cheat sheet. (Total Cool Auntie move, if I do say so myself.)

AM I ACTING LIKE A FUCKING ADULT?

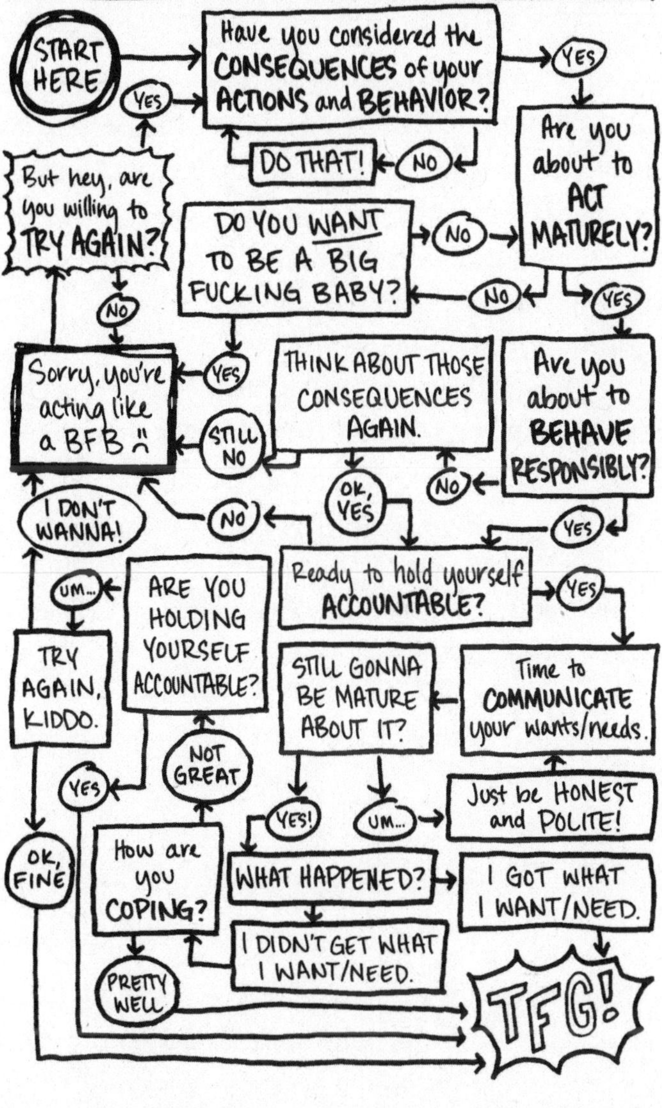

FOR MATURE
AUDIENCES ONLY:
Self-awareness, self-control, and
being on your best adult behavior

In part II, we begin from within, because how you feel — and how you *manage* how you feel — influences how you *act* on those feelz. **SELF-AWARENESS: it's a helluva drug.**

I'll open with one of the most age-old and timelessly terrifying *tut tut*s in my I'm-not-a-parent-but-I-play-one-in-this-book reper-toire: **"Do you have something to tell me?"** Longtime readers will know that **honesty has always been one of the two pillars of my No Fucks Given ethos,** and here in *Grow the Fuck Up,* we're moving beyond simply telling THE truth to focus on finding and speaking YOUR truth — **figuring out what you want and need so you can a) express it and b) achieve it.**

Then we'll touch on **integrity** — aka walking the walk after you've talked the talk — and on **recognizing and reckoning with your privilege,** before moving on to the **SELF-CONTROL** por-tion of our program, beginning with **politeness.** (That'd be NFG pillar number two, comin' in hot!)

The **"Mind your manners"** chapter is **chock-full of tips for being gracious and respectful — but also for doing it all** *strategically.* Because *you* being a pleasure to deal with makes it that much easier to subtly encourage *other people* to do your bid-ding. Trust your auntie Sarah on this. Then in **"Don't you take that tone with me,"** I'll offer practical techniques for remaining **calm, poised, articulate, and respectful** — at all times, but most especially the ones when what you really want to do is tell Janine precisely where she can shove it.

While we're on the topic of attitude adjustments, in **"I'll give you something to whine about,"** I'll help you curtail complaints before they wreck your reputation and relationships — and show you **how to vent in a much more productive way.** And we'll finish up with **"I thought I asked you not to do that,"** a lesson in the self-aware *and* self-controlled practice of **respecting other people's boundaries.**

Girl, slay!

Self-awareness

First stop on the Emotional Maturity Tour: know thyself. Because it's cute when babies start smiling on purpose instead of because they have gas, but it's even cuter when adults thoughtfully interrogate their emotions to achieve clarity on their wants and needs, so they can effectively communicate them to others! Self-awareness is knowing what you want, knowing what you have to offer, and knowing your limits. Plus, it's the ability to understand how your actions and behavior affect other people, and to adjust them accordingly. For example, if you're better able to self-assess and course-correct, then your friends won't have to *keep asking you* to stop turning every dinner conversation into a commercial for crypto, or to quit talking with your mouth full of food. Nobody wants to sit across from that.

Do you have something to tell me?

Well, do you? Come on, spit it out!

Whether it's Mom asking what became of that pie she left on the counter this morning, or your partner wanting to know why you've been so distant lately, **honesty, as the saying goes, is usually the best policy.**

For one: **it's the ethical way to fly.** If you find yourself faced with having a difficult or uncomfortable conversation, the least you can do is not be a dirty rotten liar *while* having it.

For two: **it's easier to *keep track* of the truth.** If you borrowed your roommate's favorite party dress without asking and she just found it crumpled in a heap behind the sofa where your date tossed it, it's less effort to come clean and get it dry-cleaned than to make up a tall tale about the inconsiderate intruder with a taste for strapless Zara minis. (And it would have been a LOT less effort to just ask first.)

Finally: **being a person of sound morals and strong ethics will win you more friends and influence more people than being a lying, mealymouthed prick any day of the week.**

Do you watch *Succession*? I rest my case.

But I'm not here to lecture you on telling the troof. By this point in your life, I sincerely hope you don't need Auntie Sarah to explain that lying and cheating = bad. If I wanted to spend my days harping on that basic concept, I would have married my sophomore-year college boyfriend. There was a reason my friends referred to him as "Two Thumbs Down." Yeesh.

Instead, I'd like to focus on **being honest with YOURSELF** — about how you're feeling, why you're feeling that way, and what you can do about it. **A strong sense of self-awareness is a precursor to effective interaction with others.**

I probably don't need to remind you that **Actual Babies do not have the luxury of being able to identify their emotions.** They also don't have any words for what they're feeling, critical thinking skills with which to anticipate consequences and orchestrate outcomes that would *improve* their circumstances and *change* how they're feeling, or the ability to communicate any of that shit to other people. Silly babies.

You, however, have these tools; all you need to do is use them. To that end, here's a three-step path toward becoming more self-aware — **beginning with honest *reflection* before you get to honest *expression*.**

THE HOW/WHY/WHAT METHOD
FOR FIGURING OUT, SO YOU CAN SPIT IT OUT

STEP 1:
HOW am I feeling?

STEP 2:
WHY am I feeling this way?

STEP 3:
WHAT can I do about it?

The answer to that last question may or may not involve other people, so for now, let's focus on the first two:

HOW are you feeling?
I dunno. Just kinda grumpy I suppose.

(Are you sure? Be honest!)
Wait, that wasn't one of the steps, was it? And besides, if I'm feeling it, then it's obviously true, duh!

Eh, not so fast. Part of the reason I had to write this chapter is because I encounter at least <does a quick tally> five people every day who are **extremely well versed in lying to *themselves:*** about how they're feeling and why; what's good (or bad) for them; and/or the likely consequences of their actions. It's a story as old as time.

So please humor me for a sec, put on your critical thinking cap, and dig a little deeper. It's important to **get as specific as possible with HOW** you're feeling, because that's what will **reveal the WHY** and **lead you to the most effective WHAT** [you can do about it]. For example:

Are you just kinda grumpy, or are you more specifically *overtired*? (To be fair, sleep deprivation could be making you grumpy, but we're looking to identify the root feeling/cause here.)

Are you just kinda grumpy, or are you more specifically *sad*? (Because "what action you can take" to improve a case of the grumps is not necessarily what'll help if your true state is one of grief or despair.)

Are you just kinda grumpy, or are you more specifically *hangry*? (FYI, "hungry-angry" is often *my* most successfully self-aware answer, though it took about thirty-five years for me to figure that out.)

Let's try again, shall we?

HOW are you feeling?

Actually, you know what? I am tired. REAL tired.

Okay, now that that's settled, WHY are you so tired?

I've been burning the candle at both ends for a couple of weeks, going out pretty much every night.

Good job, now do a couple more!

HOW are you feeling?

I'm sad.

WHY?

I'm lonely. I haven't seen any of my friends in a while, or even heard from anyone.

HOW are you feeling?

You know what? I'm with you. Hangry all the way.

WHY?

Because once again, I forgot to eat for nine hours straight, and now I can't even think straight. It's a problem.

Huzzah! There you go. You've taken two steps toward emotional clarity, and you're officially in the business of being more self-aware. Excellent work on all of that honest reflection. **Now we can move on to step 3: WHAT are you gonna do about it?**

HOW are you feeling?
Tired. REAL tired.

WHY?
I've been burning the candle at both ends for a couple of weeks, going out pretty much every night.

WHAT can you do about it?
I suppose I could cancel my plans for Saturday and just sleep in and keep sleeping until the sleeping is done?

Sounds like a fine idea, and I'm proud of you for figuring it out. Now **here's where "spitting it out" comes into play.**

Depending on what those Saturday plans were, you may have to tell your friends they'll need to find a sub for that Ultimate Frisbee tournament in the park, or tell your folks you need to reschedule on painting their backyard fence. In any case, **just be honest,** so you *and* everyone else can move forward as needed.

Honesty: morally sound AND efficient!

And maybe recalibrating your Saturday won't require saying anything to anybody. Like, if you were thinking about running a 10K and have now thought better of it, all you have to do is turn off your alarm and let your circadian rhythms do the rest. Easy-peasy.

Let's keep up the momentum:

HOW are you feeling?
Sad.

WHY?
I'm feeling disconnected from my friends. I haven't seen or heard from anybody lately.

WHAT can you do about it?
I could text someone and see if they want to hang out. Or even just FaceTime.

Cool, so pick up the phone and let's put an end to this sad streak. It's not like your friends can be expected to know you're feeling down and reach out at the exact right moment to lift your spirits — and hey, maybe *they're* sitting around moping and hoping to hear from *you*. Two birds, one text!

Now, one more for good measure:

HOW are you feeling?
HANGRY. SO HANGRY.

WHY?
I forgot to eat. For nine hours. Again.

WHAT can you do about it?
You're going to be so proud of me, Auntie Sarah! Before you even asked the question I was already on DoorDash ordering a Popeyes Spicy Chicken Sandwich.

PRO-DULT TIP: Gone are the days when you could rely on Mom to be carrying emergency graham crackers and string cheese in her purse for your noshing pleasure. If you're prone to hanger, note that even a pair of skinny jeans can fit enough almonds in its skinny pocket to tide you over till lunch.

Damn, kid. You are rocking and rolling. I love to see it.

PS: since this is such a fundamental method, the mastery of which I daresay most other lessons and strategies in this book will rest upon, I recommend writing it down — at least the first few times you attempt it.

HOW am I feeling?	WHY am I feeling this way?	WHAT can I do about it?
_____	_____	_____
_____	_____	_____
_____	_____	_____
_____	_____	_____
_____	_____	_____

And just like that, with three simple steps — **HOW, WHY, WHAT** — you, a mature adult, have taken the time to think more critically about your feelings than the average BFB on the block, to honestly reflect on those feelings, and to determine what actions you could take to improve your circumstances.

Often, you'll discover that those actions are easy enough to implement. **Napping, chatting, and eating: the solution to so many of life's problems!**

For the solutions that _aren't_ quite so easy — because they have higher stakes or require more nuanced communication skills than simply canceling on a picnic, texting a pal, or tipping your delivery person — never fear, as we get deeper into the book, I'll serve up plenty of **tips and techniques for having tough conversations _and_ coming out on top.**

But I'll tell you right now: the key to every single one of those convos is to **be as honest with your audience as you were with yourself.** For example:

If you're annoyed because you feel like your partner doesn't show enough interest in your career, tell them so. I've been with my husband for twenty-three years, and that's a LOT of dinner conversations to sit through, silently pissy, if you can possibly avoid it.

If you're frantic because you need your boss to give you an extra forty-eight hours to finish a task, you gotta tell them so. Unless your boss is a mentalist, they cannot read your mind. (And if they *are* a mentalist, they would already know you needed two more days, wouldn't they?)

If you're really bummed and wish your friend would shut up about ketos and calories because it sucks being dragged down into the scourge of diet culture when you're trying to enjoy a chill brunch date, THEN TELL THEM SO. Say something like "Hey, I get that this stuff is foremost in your mind, but I have to confess that it's hard for me to enjoy getting together for a meal and then spending the whole time talking about how bad it is for us or how guilty we should feel for ordering the crispy potatoes. I'm not trying to tell you how to live or relate to your own body, but if we could put a moratorium on this conversation topic while we're actively eating, I would really appreciate it. Thank you so much for understanding!"

(I promise you this is a more effective tactic than stewing in silence over your fancy shakshuka.)

---

5 things I have gotten by just fucking asking for them

Business cards
An office
A kitten
A few hours to myself
An off-menu sandwich

When you're honest about what you want and need, you are more likely to GET what you want and need. So why make it harder for everyone else to pick up what you're putting down?

It's not a lecture, peeps. It's a lifestyle.

Be your own Bad Cop

We all deserve a few free passes in this one wild and precious life, so if you get a wee bit out of hand once in a while — especially if you're the only one who gets hurt (or banned from a club) — it's not the end of the world. But it's important to try to maintain self-awareness with regard to how your behavior may be adversely affecting *other* people. Such as: realizing that you may be unintentionally dominating the conversation, and backing off a bit; or that you got a little too loud at a funeral, and taking it down a notch; or that your dirty sense of humor is not jiving with the guests at your dad's retirement party, and toning it down...a lot. And free passes aside, if someone has to ask you once to simmer down (or has to stab your leg under the table to stop you from reciting that filthy punch line), don't make them ask/stab you twice. Total Fucking Grownups take the hint.

Talking the talk AND walking the walk

Part of being self-aware is honestly assessing and expressing your wants and needs. But you've also got to back that shit up: by **acting in line with the words that came out of your mouth, following through on promises, and enforcing boundaries.** Like when you asked your nonmentalist boss for that extension; if they grant it, then you're on the hook to use the extra time wisely and deliver on your new deadline. Or, for example:

> If HOW you were feeling was pissed off and WHY was because the other guys in your band promised you were going to get a solo in the last show and then yoinked it at the last minute because they said you weren't quite ready yet, and WHAT

you decided to do about it was double down on rehearsal time, then that was very mature of you. Well done! And now — if and when you *do* get another shot to shred — it's up to you to remain worthy *of* that chance by continuing to hold yourself to the same standard that you asked the guys to recognize.

Or, let's say HOW you're feeling is ashamed, WHY is because you really misbehaved toward your family, and WHAT you decided to do about it was honestly, humbly ask their forgiveness. Again, v. mature. Just note that if you've managed to rally someone back onto your side with a seemingly sincere apology, a great way to *keep* them on your side is to keep your word and keep up the good behavior.

And if you've asked for what you want and need and *also* indicated what you're capable of giving in return, then wow, your self-awareness knows no bounds!

For example, perhaps you did manage to honestly spit it out when your partner asked why you were being so distant lately. You told them HOW you were feeling (unhappy in the relationship); WHY (because it seems like you have to do everything to keep your household running); and WHAT you've decided to do about it (ask them to contribute more to chores, planning, or other emotional labor, or you may have to reconsider this whole "partnership" thing entirely). Great job talking the talk. I know that wasn't easy. But you still have to walk the walk — and not get walked all over — which may mean enforcing the consequences you so honestly laid out. If they can't get their shit together, that's on them; but if you can't stick to your expressed boundaries, then all of that short-term success at speaking your truth becomes a failure of fortitude in the long run.

When it comes to honest communication and maintaining your integrity, it's never too late to turn yourself from a person who mumbles and dissembles and flails and bails into **someone who speaks their truth AND backs it up with their actions.**

We've all been guilty of doing the opposite. In some cases, it was because we genuinely didn't know better. We didn't yet have the self-awareness, the words to express it, or the courage of our convictions. And that's okay, but those aren't — or at least, shouldn't be — evergreen excuses.

Because you can *accumulate* the self-awareness and *practice* the words and *summon* the courage of your convictions, if you really want to.

And you're still reading, so I'd say you're ahead of the game.

Look both ways

Speaking of "ahead of the game," I'd like to close out our saga of self-awareness **with a brief discussion of privilege.**

Communicating politely, kindly, and respectfully is a big part of the rest of part II. But doing so *while* checking your privilege — to uncover potential prejudices and/or blind spots that could lead to unsavory behavior — is **another level of self-awareness and maturity that's worth highlighting, even if it might make you a little uncomfortable.**

Folks: I have been there, I have stepped in it, and I get it. And I'm still making mistakes and trying to learn from them. But it's precisely *because* I wish so much that someone had had this conversation with me earlier in life that I want to touch upon it here, in hopes of shedding some light for anyone else who may be struggling to understand the concept of their own privilege, or be unaware of it entirely.

For my part, in addition to being white, straight, and cisgender, I've also benefited from a stable family unit and access to higher education, and am fortunate to have a lucrative career, a strong marriage, and more. The only way I could have *more* privilege is if I were a dude, but I'm running a strong second here.

I know that now, but I didn't always.

And I cringe to think about the regrettable (and unfortunately, rather public) arguments I've gotten into in the past that stemmed from my failure to understand what privilege is — beyond simply having money or status — and how mine has served me in so many ways. The best I can do is hold those interactions up as teachable moments, so here we are.

If my personal experience is any guide, I think one of the reasons people get defensive when the P-word comes into play is that **they feel like acknowledging they *have it* somehow makes them seem less "deserving"** of things they worked hard to achieve.

But here's the rub: privilege doesn't mean you haven't worked hard to achieve things. It means that *who you are* hasn't made achieving those things *harder*.

Race, sexuality, gender, socioeconomic status, physical ability, and even geography can limit or enhance a person's access to resources and opportunity. So you may have worked superduper hard indeed, but you also may have done that work on **a playing field that was tilted considerably in your favor.**

(You may also have *not* worked terribly hard and *still* gotten ahead, and that could *definitely* be the result of privilege you may or may not realize you have.)

And — again, in my experience — another way that people expose their lack of awareness of their own privilege happens when **they *think* they're being supportive (and even progressive!) in their expressed views,** without realizing that the effect of what they're saying or doing is actually quite the opposite.

An example might be a straight, cis person telling a privately out but publicly closeted queer or trans friend to "Just come out! We all love you, and this is the twenty-first century, nobody cares!"

If you've ever done that, you might have thought you were being a good friend, and even truly believed what you said — precisely because who YOU are doesn't make it harder to access civil rights like marriage, or basic human rights like gender-affirming care, so you're just not connecting the dots. And **that lack of self-awareness can be hurtful on a personal front, as well as damaging on a larger scale** when it comes to situations like hiring, teaching, policing, or voting with your blinders on.

If you are someone who possesses a distinct *lack* of privilege — with less access to fewer resources with which to accomplish your goals; or who hasn't been given the opportunity to reach for those goals in the first place — I know enough to know that I'll never truly understand how difficult and frustrating and hurtful that is for you. But I hope these pages go some small way toward making you feel seen, and to moving the conversations about equity and equality forward for your more privileged peers.

In any case, if you're serious about becoming a mature, self-aware, Total Fucking Grownup, **it's on you to accept these realities and put them into context.**

Checking your privilege isn't only about having empathy and compassion for others. It may begin there, but it must lead to **interrogating your own place in the world;** understanding that you may have baked-in advantages; being willing to admit that your *unawareness* of those advantages may have caused you to act or behave in a way that hurt someone else, or a group of people; and, most importantly, being willing to change.

As I've become more aware of my own privilege, I've tried to change the way I think, talk about, and act on issues like race and gender identity, as well as trying to make the effort to speak up when I see other people making the same missteps I have.

And guess what? **It's hard to stop being who you've always been and saying what you've always said in the way you've always said it!** And even harder to point out complicated, uncomfortable stuff to other people. Still gotta do it, though.

Reckoning with privilege is a challenge, and rising to that challenge requires **a willingness to look both ways: AT your own experience and also OUTSIDE of it.** You can get started by seeking out perspectives from people who are different from you — an easy and accessible way to self-educate.

Follow new-to-you voices on social media, or **related hashtags** (e.g., #blacklivesmatter or #transrightsarehuman rights) that will automatically populate your feeds with new and different POVs.

Check out articles, books, or podcasts that expose you to unfamiliar issues explored by the people who are living with and through them.

Then consider how your experience compares. Ask yourself whether, based on what you've learned, you occupy a privileged place in society? And if so, use that new understanding to inform your actions and behavior going forward.

It's extraordinarily valuable to open up your world view, at any age. I hope you'll join me in that pursuit, and that wherever you are in your adulting journey — and whether it's over dinner with old friends or online among strangers — you'll commit to being more self-aware about what you're thinking and saying and how your level of privilege and that of those around you play into all of it.

And look, you don't know what you don't know. That's just how it is sometimes, and it's okay. As someone who was thirty-nine years old when she learned that a spirit animal is a sacred totem, and not a phrase that a non–Native American should be co-opting in an Instagram caption (or anywhere else), I have no business lecturing anybody on what they "should have known" and when.

But I will say this:

Once you DO know it? Own it. And do better.

Self-control

Now that you've gotten a handle on *assessing* how you feel and what you need, you can move toward *expressing* it in the most mature and strategic fashion — including and especially when you're feeling fed up, fucked over, or put-upon. Keeping your composure in those situations is more likely to result in *actual progress toward your goal,* which ought to outweigh the initial burst of satisfaction that may come from stomping, spitting, or slamming your way onto someone's permanent blacklist. The short-term gains are clear, and building your reputation as a cool customer will serve you again and again over the long haul.

Mind your manners

Politeness has always been the second stalwart pillar of my No Fucks Given oeuvre. And as with that other pillar, honesty, I hope it goes without saying that **we should all be out here being polite because it's the right thing to do.**

Say *please* when you want something, *thank you* when you get something, and throw in a *you're welcome* when someone else does the right thing and thanks YOU. If you want to tack a "sir" or "ma'am" on there at the end, that can be a nice touch, but do be mindful when using gender-specific honorifics. Calling someone by their actual name is an excellent alternative to accidentally misgendering them, and if you don't know their name, all you have to do is ask. (Or look to see if it's displayed on a tag clipped to their shirt.)

Anyway, WOO! **Give it up for basic human decency!**

But if you're looking for even more GTFU MO-tivation, check this out: **being polite is more than just an altruistic pursuit; it's also a *strategic* one.** Magnanimous manners-minding will up your R&R levels in a consistent, significant way. And if that sounds icky or baldly transactional to you, consider this:

How does it make *you* feel when someone treats you with kindness, consideration, and respect? How are you inclined to respond to and reward that behavior?

Alternatively, when someone interrupts you, ignores you, or constantly points out your failures and ignores your triumphs, what does that do for ya?

The Golden Rule says "Do unto others as you would have them do unto you." (I didn't make that up; it's from the Bible, which you may be shocked to learn that your potty-mouthed guru has read, beginning to end. What can I say? I like to keep you on your toes.) And when it comes to being polite, following ye olde GR results in two big wins that have lovely ramifications for your everyday life:

1. When you're polite, people LIKE you more.

Now, perhaps in your heart of hearts you don't really care whether people like you, which: Same, girl. Same. But regardless, the trickle-down benefits of being well liked are numerous and well documented — and being polite is *so* easy — it seems like a no-brainer to just roll with it. For example:

- **Want to make a good impression on potential future in-laws?** Speak kindly to them *and* to their treasured dachshund, Reginald. Observe traditional rules of etiquette (e.g., come bearing a small gift, compliment their home, send a thank-you note for the lovely brunch) along with less traditional ones such as "no loud sex on the sofa bed" and "don't stink up the bathroom if you can possibly avoid it." In case of emergency, a travel-sized bottle of Poo-Pourri is your friend, friend.

- **Wish you had a little more support at work?** If you make a habit of complimenting your colleague's way with a PowerPoint, I bet they'll be feeling awfully darn appreciated and useful the day you have to lean on them for help in polishing a presentation of your own.

PRO-DULT TIP: I don't know who needs to hear this, but if you spend the weekend (or longer) at someone else's house, you ought to — bare minimum — offer to cook, do dishes, or pay for a round of takeout or groceries; wipe down the sink and shower of your toothpaste and hair; and strip the bed before you leave. Even if your friends have a cleaning service or protest that "it's no trouble at all" to have you here, ADULTS STRIP THE MOTHERFUCKING BED.

- **Got friends with a nice lake house where you enjoy spending three-day weekends?** Be a gracious guest, you get invited back. (And you get the best room.)

When people like you, they're more likely to
Fit you in when they're "fully booked"
Invite you as their plus-one to an awesome party
Cut you some slack when you *do* misbehave
Let down their guard and just be chill (always useful with in-laws!)

2. **When you're polite, people RESPECT you more.**

Likability is one thing; respectability is a whole other bag of chips. And no matter how you feel about the former, I highly recommend encouraging the latter, which leads down a pretty sweet two-way street. For example:

- **Looking to make your travel day more pleasant?** Being respectful toward the gate agents and flight attendants is a surefire way to get on their radar as "not an asshole," which could result in a better seat, a second snack, or an extra strong G&T — while the disrespectful clown in front of you gets the "random" extra security screening and the warmest bottle of white wine on board.

- **Want to make the most of your entry-level position?** Showing the utmost respect for your colleagues and managers proves you can be trusted to be dignified and discreet, and could result in you being invited earlier and more often to sit in on high-level meetings and meet influential contacts.

- **Hoping your partner will agree to make a big move or a change they're not yet comfortable with?** Take the time to respectfully listen to their concerns and demonstrate your willingness to work through them. Not feeling heard can sometimes be the biggest hurdle of all.

Yup. **ALL OF THIS AND MORE COULD BE YOURS.** Especially if you're willing to branch out into even more impressive (and equally easy) forms of politesse beyond *please* and *thank you*.

> **When people respect you, they're more likely to**
>
> Trust you
> Support you
> Fear you (Hey, it's a perk.)
> Leave you the fuck alone to do your job

Transactional? Fine, but not in an icky "I'm taking advantage of anybody" way; just in an "I'm following the Golden Rule, and if that gives someone else a subliminal push to do the same, then it works out well for both of us" way. If it's in the Bible, how wrong could it be?*

6 Extra-Impressive and Equally Easy Ways to Be Polite, Beyond Saying *Please* and *Thank you*

Be quiet

Here's a neat trick: you can be polite without saying a word! Actual Babies babble and scream no matter who has the floor. Big Fucking Babies leave their ringers on during movies and talk over you in meetings. Even Theoretical Adults sometimes can't resist whispering to a neighbor. (WE CAN HEAR YOU, MARSHA.) But **Total Fucking Grownups know that silence is golden.** They don't interrupt. They listen when others are speaking; sit still when people are performing; and zip their lips when Auntie Sarah is clearly pausing for effect and not looking for input from the crowd. Much appreciated.

---

* Don't answer that.

Bite your tongue

Another mode of "being quiet" is the classic **"If you don't have anything nice to say, don't say anything at all"** approach to winning friends and influencing people. (I cannot tell you how

Polite alternatives to *Please*
May I?
Shall we?
Would you mind terribly?
Could I be so bold as to request?
<kneel and genuflect>

much *less* polite my friends, family, and colleagues would consider me if I made a habit of saying out loud everything that's marinating in the darkest folds of my cerebrum. Yowza.) To illustrate this point, consider the following scenarios:

> Your friend proudly announces their plan for becoming a certified baby-goat-yoga instructor. You, a Theoretical Adult with a politeness deficiency, do a spit take with your coffee, laugh, and say, "You're joking, right?"

OR

> You, a Total Fucking Grownup, swallow your java, widen your eyes in the universal signal for "Isn't that neat!" and watch silently as your pal happily diagrams their new backyard goat pen.

✳

Your roommate is hanging posters of Willem Dafoe all over their bedroom wall. Like, a lot of fucking posters of Willem Dafoe. You, an immature bébé, snicker when you see this happening, and say, "Um, *seriously* with the Green Goblin? Do you have a freaky-old-dude fetish or something?"

OR

You, a mature adult, say NOT A GODDAMN WORD and just let Dafoes hang where they may, because it doesn't affect your life one bit, and also kink-shaming is not cool.

✳

Your supervisor unveils a startlingly dumb slogan to encourage teamwork and boost productivity. Something like: IF WE CAN DREAM IT, WE CAN TEAM IT! You, a borderline BFB, retreat to the office Slack channel to make immature jokes at the boss's expense, forgetting about a little thing called "screenshots." (Not to mention "coworkers with zero loyalty to you.")

OR

You, a mature, respectful TFG, simply nod and smile and go back to work — thinking all the snarky, disparaging thoughts your lizard brain can generate, but never, *ever* committing them to print.

You see where I'm going here. Putting people down isn't necessary, and it certainly isn't nice. Plus, someday you might need a goat's milk hookup, or for your roomie or your boss to turn a blind eye to a peccadillo of your own. When that day comes, you'll be glad you learned to hold your tongue instead of letting it loose it all over town.

Be complimentary

Prioritize giving credit where credit is due. Lobbing out praise for a job well done or a party well planned or a turkey well brined

Polite alternatives to *Thank you*
I am much obliged.
You're the best!
Bless you.
You're an angel sent from heaven.
<compose grateful haiku>

should always be your default response when presented with the fruits of someone else's labor. Keep a few go-to polite compliments in your back pocket and you'll be everyone's favorite guest, teammate, coworker, and family member in no time. For example:

"Hey, great job today!"

"I'm a real fan of your work."

"I see what you did there, and I appreciate it."

"You really make this shit look easy."

"This might be the best [insert homemade food item] I've ever had!"

"My Lord, that ass!"

Not all compliments are created equal. In the grand tradition of "think before you speak," please take a moment to be sure that whatever nicety you think you're conveying is *actually nice* and not weirdly offensive — such as invoking someone's past failures to "compliment" their recent success ("Oh wow, I never thought you'd get into grad school with those grades. Congrats!") or employing toxic tropes to comment on their appearance. There's a fine line between "You look great" and "Allow me to objectify your body and/or imply that there was something wrong with you before you lost weight/went on Accutane/grew out your bangs." Actually, you know what? It's not a fine line. It's a thick and obvious one and easy to not cross, so don't.

Be diplomatic

If you must argue a point or point out a flaw, you should resist the urge to lecture, hector, or demean — and that goes for best friends, bosses, and everyone in between. Unless you're specifically gunning for Gordon Ramsay's Food Network gig, you're better off holding your temper and approaching conflict with an even hand. I'll go into more detail on *how* to turn down the heat a bit later in **"Don't you take that tone with me,"** but here are a few examples to get your tactful tactics in fighting form:

WHAT YOU'RE THINKING	WHAT YOU COULD SAY INSTEAD
Wow, you are the stupidest person I know.	"You may want to consider another angle on this."
You could not be more wrong.	"Let me lay out some facts that might change some things for you."
Fuck you and the horse you rode in on.	"I confess I see this issue a bit differently. Let's discuss?"

(And one more thing — I'm all for being sincerely deferential, but let's steer clear of those faux-polite intros "With all due respect" and "No offense, but…" I think we all know nobody ever started a sentence like that and actually meant it.)

Be considerate

Readers of my books *The Life-Changing Magic of Not Giving a Fuck* and *Fuck No!* know that I'm a big fan of being able to do what you want — and *not* do what you *don't* want — as long as you're polite about it. For example, however you intend to RSVP to an invitation, send that reply in a timely fashion. It's rude to leave someone hanging when they've got an entire party to plan, budget for, and execute, and all *you* have to do is check a fucking box on an Evite.

(It's also rude to bail at the last minute without a good reason. So if you don't have one of those, at least be considerate enough to fake an airtight alibi, ya baby.)

If you do intend to attend an event by adults, for adults, *remain* considerate by respecting the guest list, the start time, the end time, and the overall scene. There's a time and a place for bringing plus-ones (or plus-tens) and passing out wasted on your host's futon at the end of the night, and that time is in your early twenties at a loft party. TFGs

know when it's appropriate — and when IT MOST CERTAINLY IS NOT — to bring a guest (or a child, or a pet), or to waltz in late or peace out early.

And if they have one too many and throw up on your duvet, an adult has the wherewithal to apologize immediately and profusely, and get it dry-cleaned without being asked. Which means they have a decent shot at being invited back, because **Total Fucking Grownups also know this: you can be forgiven for a LOT of *faux pas* if you make the effort to be considerate about them.**

Need to cancel plans? Do it as soon as you can.

Unfortunately, it's a last-minute thing? Own up to any inconvenience you've caused, and apologize.

Can't get it up to mail a thank-you note? Fine, but surely you can send a nice text.

Can't make a deadline? Give your boss/client/coworker a heads-up ASAP.

Going to be late on rent? Ditto, kiddo.

And in true "saving the best for last" style...

Be kind

Hold the door for a harried neighbor. Offer the UPS driver a drink of water. Give up your seat on the bus or your spot in line to someone who seems like they need it more. **Performing random acts of kindness will make you feel good, and it'll make other people feel good *about you,* too.**

That's a win-fucking-win for the ages.

Yes, my pets. Your friends and family, coworkers, gate agents, and dates will appreciate that you're a mature adult who is not only *pleasey-thanky,* but also quietly respectful, complimentary, diplomatic, considerate, and kind — and I have it on high authority that you'll get those positive vibes back in return.

I mean, I use all of the right words and none of the bad hand gestures, and I'm here to tell you that Auntie Sarah tends to get what she wants out of life (and front-desk clerks).

You can call it transactional if you want to, but you *cannot* tell me that shit doesn't work.

Don't you take that tone with me

Alrighty. Having cautioned you against being rude, now we're gonna work on your mood and improve your 'tude. Welcome to the **COPING** part of the C-Cycle, where tantrums fear to tread!

You will not always get what you want. This is one of the more brutal lessons you learn as you get older, and when it lands, **the grownup way to express your disappointment** — ensuring the best outcome and least blowback for YOU — is to remain:

CALM

POISED

ARTICULATE

and

RESPECTFUL

In this chapter I'll give you a bunch of strategies for getting there, and **maturely maintaining your self-control when the going gets cranky.** But first, and since part of my charm is the way I remain down-to-earth and accessible even as I dictate sage advice to the masses, I thought I'd share **a cautionary tale about a time when Auntie Sarah forgot her ABCs** and did not cope with the fallout very well at all, no she did not.

And then we'll talk about what I could (and should) have done differently.

The calm before the tweetstorm

Many years ago (although not so many that I have any excuse for my immature behavior), I was involved in a professional transaction that went awry. I'll spare you the details; they're not especially relevant and trying to explain the ins and outs of the publishing biz would run counter to my goal of making this book *snappy.* Suffice it to say, I felt I'd been wronged and I proceeded to do the least adult thing in the world: I took to Twitter with my grievance.

I stopped short of naming names, but still, rookie mistake. After tweeting my bitchy blind item, I drank a[nother] glass of wine and went to bed.

When I got to work the next morning, I found a couple of sheets of paper sitting on my desk chair, and as I picked them up and read them, my stomach did a flip-flop worthy of Simone Biles on floor exercise. The top page was a printout of an email exchange between the person I had grumbled about on Twitter — who recognized themselves in my pissy little tweetstorm, even if no one else could have — and MY BOSS, to whom my nemesis had tattled that one of his direct reports was acting like a grade-A brat on the interwebs.

The second page was a printout of the tweets in question. "Come see me when you get in" was scrawled across the top in blue pen. *Fuuuuuck.*

Thankfully, up to this point I'd had an excellent track record in being a mature, responsible employee, so my juvenile indiscretion was treated as "strike one" rather than "you're out." Still, I suffered a squirmy sit-down with my boss and I'm VERY VERY LUCKY that it all didn't go much worse.

Trust me, kids, this is not a wheel you wish to spin.

So with that cautionary tale in mind, let's take it back to the first of those four grownup ways to cope with and express your disappointment: staying **CALM.**

It's time to self-soothe, my dudes.

No fussin'

In child development–speak, self-soothing is when a baby puts themselves to sleep (or *back* to sleep) with no intervention or encouragement from a caregiver — and ideally without too much crying, kicking, or screaming, for everybody's sake. Though if you ask me, the "self" part is a bit of a misnomer, since before Baby even lifts a wrinkly little finger to hit SNOOZE, it's *the adults around them* who've had to do the work of "establishing a routine" and "investing in a white noise machine" and "crafting DIY blackout shades out of aluminum foil so the sun can't fuck this up for all of us."*

Anyway, regardless, and as we have already established: YOU are not a baby. So here in *Grow the Fuck Up*, we're going to talk about some actual "self"-soothing techniques that'll help hone your ability to **process difficult emotions in a mature, healthy, and productive way.**

When you find yourself in need of a little worst-impulses control, here are **three tips for remaining calm and keeping your cool** — not to mention keeping your job, your relationships, and your self-respect.

---

* I have helped a mom friend do this. It was BANANAS.

Put *yourself* in "time-out"

When I was in nursery school, going on a "time-out" meant being sent to sit in the corner and think about whatever it was you did that got you sent there. As punishments go it was mild, given that it allowed you the space to calm down, reflect, and maybe even pick your nose in peace. Today, we're going to use it **not as a punishment, but as a preventative measure.**

Per our earlier exercise in HOW/WHY/WHAT, let's say you've identified HOW you're feeling as "pissed off," WHY as "because you're being tragically undervalued at work," and WHAT you've done to address it is "summoned the courage to ask for a promotion." Good on ya! Unfortunately, your supervisor got back to you with some version of "That's not happening." Or maybe they've been studiously ignoring you for a week. Either way you're not getting what you want, you still feel pissed off/undervalued, and now you're mad *and* all kinds of primed to clap back in an ill-advised way.

HOWEVER! You are not a baby; you are a goddamn adult with excellent taste in self-help books. So instead of sending a "WTF" email or ambushing your absentee boss in the restroom — neither of which is likely to result in a good outcome — you're going to take a *preventative* time-out.

That's right, bud. I want you to go stand in the real or metaphorical corner and **silently recite your ABCs until your self is muthafuckin' SOOTHED.**

> *My actions and behavior have consequences.*

> *My actions and behavior have consequences.*

> *My actions and behavior have consequences.*

Then, when you think you might be ready to issue a mature response, THINK AGAIN, and keep my next tip in mind to keep your foot out of your mouth. (Another thing babies cannot be trusted to do. Dummies.)

The Triple O

In workplace lingo, **"OOO" stands for "Out of Office."** This is when you set up an automatic response in your email program that lets people know they won't be hearing back from you right away — because you're on vacation, on parental leave, out sick, or whatever. The gist is "I am not here, I haven't seen your message, and you won't receive a reply until I'm back and I do." And even in the work-first culture of the USA, most colleagues, clients, bosses, and randos popping up in your inbox are conditioned to take an OOO at face value.

So I say, why not take a page from that highly successful "Not today, Satan!" delay tactic and apply it *whenever* you need a little more time and space before responding in full, whether in a professional OR personal situation?

The next time someone burns your biscuits, instead of tearing into them like a stoner with a midnight bag of Taco Bell, try this little trick:

Blink twice (as though the motherboard in your brain just received the "bounce-back" instruction) and say something like, **"Ah, okay, I'm occupied with some other stuff right now, so let me get back to you when I have the bandwidth."** Or if you are not a person who can unironically use the phrase "when

I have the bandwidth," substitute "when I come up for air."

Whatever! Make it your own.

The point is, **the Triple O keeps you from "O"-verreacting in the moment.** And again, this tip is not limited to workplace usage.

For example, say you're an adult juggling adult duties like working a full day and getting home in time for the four-hour window to wait for the cable guy, during which dinner must be made, dishes done, you have to call and check in on Dad to see how he's recovering from last week's surgery — oh, and let's add "make the grocery list for tomorrow because if you don't do it now you'll wind up shopping hangry and wasting your food budget on Pop-Tarts and beef jerky."

Midway through executing this stunning feat of adulting, your best friend calls to lay upon you a crisis resulting from the predictable consequences of their own [decidedly nongrownup] actions. You're feeling kind of besieged, but you wouldn't want to take your lack of bandwidth out on your friend by screaming "Leave me alone!" and throwing metaphorical sand in their eyes the way you might have handled this back in kindergarten. You want to be polite and considerate, but also postpone this convo until you're damn well ready to have it.

So use your brain like you'd use Outlook or Gmail and call up an appropriately benign response that will serve to put the whole scenario on pause while you catch your breath. Something like, **"I'm sorry but this is a really bad time. Let me call you back tomorrow, okay? Love you, byeeee!"**

<Click>

Your turn: as an exercise, write down a few go-to replies or phrasing that you could employ to slow your reactionary roll. (Personally, I love a good "Noted!" as my initial email/text/in-person response. One word, polite, and makes no promises.)

_____

_____

Sometimes, a well-timed time-out and/or an expertly executed Triple O are all you need to tamp down a rising tantrum — and then you can **move on to expressing yourself effectively, using the rest of this chapter's tips.** Awesome. But other times, you may wish to try one more calming strategy that could save you the trouble of having to express yourself at all…

Just fucking let it go

One of my most popular nuggets of NFG wisdom comes from my book *Calm the Fuck Down.* I call it the **One Question to Rule Them All:** *Can I control it?* If the answer is no, you need to let it go.

When reacting/responding to someone who's done you wrong, the One Q can help you cut through the noise, stop freaking out about shit you have no control over (aka relief), and focus productively on other things that bring joy and order to your life (aka reward).

Ask yourself whether engaging with your antagonist is likely to improve your situation, or make it worse. What are the consequences here? Is there really anything you can say to orchestrate a better outcome for yourself, or would you just be wasting time and energy slamming your head against a brick dickface?

Can you control this situation? No? Then you know what to do.*

Letting it go is the adultiest of moves. I understand that it may seem easier said than done, but if it helps you take the plunge, just know that there is no better feeling in the world than depriving some brick dickface of the satisfaction of seeing you break.

Now, let's say you've timed out, Triple O'd, calmly determined that this situation IS one in which you may be able to exert control toward a potentially positive and satisfying outcome, and you DO wish to respond — well then, let's get you **POISED** for lift-off.

---

5 ways to let it go

Literally walk away
Download a meditation
    app
Actually use the
    meditation app
Eat a cookie (it's harder to
    say stupid shit with your
    mouth full)
one word: microdose

---

* In Auntie Sarah's case, she should have skipped Twitter and gone straight to the tub.

Stand up straight, and no fidgeting

If "calm" is your interior state, then think of **"poised" as your exterior state — your mind-set translated into your physical presence.**

Once again, I invite you to consider the difference between an Actual Baby and a Total Fucking Grownup, both of whom have a legitimate grievance. One of them is likely to get red in the face, shake with uncontrollable fury, and possibly fling their own mucus at the offending party, while the other is capable of speaking in a well-modulated tone punctuated by nary a stray booger. Here are three tips for staying on the mature, productive, and effective side of that comparison:

Take a deep breath

It's a cliché, but if you want to avoid getting all wobbly, wiggly, and crazy-eyed when you have the chance to say your piece, there is no faster, easier way to Zen out before-hand than by using the lungs your mama gave you — to breathe, not to scream. **Breathe in through your nose for four, out through your mouth for six. Repeat as needed.**

The great thing about deep-breathing exercises is they don't take long to have a positive effect, and you can do them anywhere: at your desk, in your car, in an elevator, stairwell, or restroom, or hovering by a rack of hoodies at the Gap. (I'm not saying I once worked across the street from a Gap to which I may or may not have frequently escaped on my lunch break in order to breathe myself into fighting shape for an afternoon showdown with a certain colleague, but I'm not *not* saying that either.)

Strike a Power Pose

Amy Cuddy popularized this strategy in her book *Presence: Bringing Your Boldest Self to Your Biggest Challenges*. Some folks attacked her claims about the link between how we hold our bodies and how we think and feel about ourselves as "pseudoscience," but I for one am here to tell you that that shit worked for me in a major way. (And also that Power Poses — essentially, puffing out your chest, lifting your arms high and wide, and strutting around with purpose — look and feel just as weird as you think they do.)

I did them backstage before giving my TEDx Talk on "The Magic of Not Giving a F*ck," which I nailed. I credit

80 percent of that performance to preparation (see next tip) and 18 percent to Power Poses.*

> **Note: this technique is not limited to public speaking.** No, ma'am! You can do Power Poses before an important meeting, a negotiation, a first date, a breakup conversation, or anytime you want to walk into a situation feeling bigger, taller, stronger, and more badass. Or you can do them in your living room when your book is due in one week and the impostor syndrome has kicked into high gear. Again, not that I would know anything about that.

Dress for success

To nail the poise part of our equation, give extra consideration to your battle armor, and choose something that will help you feel more confident going into this showdown. It could be anything from your lucky jumpsuit to a statement jacket or a pair of don't-fuck-with-me heels. (Maybe all three, if you're Timothée Chalamet.) And remember, it's not about how you look, but rather, how you *feel* about

---

* The other 2 percent goes to Xanax, obvs.

how you look that translates into a poised persona. It doesn't matter what anybody else thinks — and if this particular battle is taking place over the phone and they can't see you at all, then your outfit qualifies as a secret weapon. Even better.

So that's **POISE.** Deep breaths. Stand up straight. Chest out, dressed to kill — or just for comfort; truly, whatever makes you feel your bodily best!

The next step?

Use your words

When you're ready to actively communicate your self-aware feelings and needs, the good news is: you don't need a master's degree in oratory and rhetoric to make an effective point or win an argument. You don't even need to learn any four-syllable words, I promise. **You just need to be ARTICULATE.**

(Okay, that's a four-syllable word, but it's just a fancy way of saying "speak clearly." I was an English major; I can't help myself.)

Anyway, all I'm saying is, don't get cute. **Talking out of your ass will only land you out of your depth,** and then anyone wiser and more informed — and with better communication skills — will run circles around you and send you back to square one.

Instead, focus on **giving the clearest, most coherent delivery of the words you *do* know,** which will be much more effective than nonsensically jibber-jabbering away like a toddler or a certain tangerine-hued president of the United States of America, neither of whom anyone in the history of time has ever described as "articulate."

The same goes for more intimate conversations. **Keep. It. Simple.**

For example, if it's time to have a capital-T talk with the person you're dating, remember your HOW/WHY/WHAT Method for figuring it out so you can spit it out, and deliver the "WHAT" in an honest *and* straightforward way.

Use YOUR words, reflective of YOUR feelings and YOUR needs/goals — not a bunch of technical mumbo-jumbo you found when you Googled "Is my partner an emotional cripple?" After all, if you don't even know what you're talking about, how will they?

And if you're worried about being able to **organize your thoughts into an articulate whole, that's what notebooks and voice recorders and draft emails/texts are for!** You don't have to prepare a monologue on the spot like you're early-2000s Eminem at a rap battle. Just map everything out beforehand so you can show up calm, poised, *and* prepared.

Finally, when it comes to **establishing the appropriate and most effective rapport** with whoever's on the other end of your devastatingly articulate argument, **you need to show a little R-E-S-P-E-C-T if you expect to get any R-E-S-P-E-C-T.**

Do you kiss Beyoncé with that mouth?

My last tip for **coping-slash-communicating like a TFG** is to treat everybody like you'd treat Queen Bey.

IF YOU DON'T THINK IT WOULD BE WISE TO TAKE THAT TONE AND USE THOSE WORDS WITH HER, THEN DON'T TAKE IT/USE THEM WITH YOUR BOSS, BOYFRIEND, PROFESSOR, PROBLEM CUSTOMER, THAT LADY WHO CUT YOU IN LINE, THE BOUNCER AT THE BAR, OR ANYONE ELSE.

I'm telling you, you'll catch more flies with honey, and you're also much less likely to get attacked by your sister-in-law in an elevator after the Met Gala.

And keep in mind that **showing respect is not limited to**

the words you choose; it's also about when and how you wield them, which could help your cause on a personal level and avoid hurting it on a strategic one. You may want to pause and check your privilege, or take a gander beyond your immediate needs to consider other people's extenuating circumstances. For example:

If your objective is financial remuneration, remember that you can't squeeze blood from a stone. A Fortune 500 company that hasn't given you a cost-of-living increase in three years? Go for the jugular. A roommate who owes you grocery money but has fallen on hard times? Lead with compassion.

If your beef is with a busy working parent, and you're hoping for a receptive audience, maybe don't reach out during the hours of "getting everybody ready for school" or "family dinnertime."

If you have a sensitive bone to pick with someone, do it discreetly. The group text/Slack channel is no place for private pissing matches.

If this is a professional sitch, remember who you're dealing with — i.e., a person who stamps your pay stubs — and interact with them accordingly. (And definitely don't refer to it as a "sitch" when you ask to set up the meeting.)

In other words: respect people's time, their limitations, and their dignity. And respect the pecking order too. **A big part of growing the fuck up is understanding how the world operates, and learning how to work the system instead of letting the system work YOU.**

And now, for the penultimate chapter of part II, we'll be combining fuss-free communication and productive coping techniques all in one, on a little tour of whine country.*

I'll give you something to whine about

First, I should say that blowing off steam is a perfectly valid pursuit. That valve that releases pent-up air so your Instant Pot doesn't explode all over the kitchen? It's a feature, not a bug!

But whining *all* the time and just for the hell or attention of it are hallmarks of literal and figurative Big Fucking Babies — and no one wants to spend their days in the presence of either a small

---

* These are the jokes, folks.

child OR a grown-ass adult who is **constantly irritated, never satisfied, and won't shut up about it.**

Then there are those of us with legitimate gripes and a legitimate need to express them in exchange for some much-needed emotional relief. All well and good — like I said, vent away! — unless and until you find yourself *only* venting and never *doing anything* **to address the root cause of your complaints.**

That's inching back toward "just for the hell or attention of it" territory, which, as discussed, is not a good look.

For example, let's say you have a difficult boss, and you tend to unload about them every time you meet up with friends for drinks. Also every time you talk to your parents. And whenever you can intercept the coworker who shares your cubicle wall. Oh, and that person you've been dating? They get an earful about Hellboss a couple of times a week — over dinner, on the way to the movies, and in bed.

It's…a LOT.

And although your friends and family may be among your biggest fans, they didn't sign up for lifetime, front-row seats to your one-person show *Everything Sucks!*. Your coworkers' job descriptions definitely do not include "listening to you bellyache all day." And while every romantic relationship thrives on healthy communication — which includes being there for one another when times are tough — if complaining is your love language, don't be surprised if dinner dates get cut short or someone starts sleeping on the couch. Or elsewhere entirely.

But I'll tell you a secret for those of us who love — nay, *need* — a good bitch sesh from time to time: **if you're willing to put a productive spin on your problems, it's possible to have your kvetch and eat it too.**

With regard to Hellboss, for example, how about you get your necessary steam release on **while asking for help in brainstorming ways to improve your circumstances?** I'm sure your aforementioned biggest fans would be more than happy to participate in such a conversation if it means you can eventually stop suffering through this shit and then *EVERYONE* CAN STOP FUCKING TALKING ABOUT IT.

Does one of your friends (or even a friend of a friend) work in your industry, and might they know about job openings at their company? Network that shit!

Perhaps your dad has a few insights from his long career as a corporate worker bee that could help you put things in perspective, handle your boss more effectively, and be less aggravated on the daily?

Instead of griping your way through Happy Hour, could you make an appointment with HR? If your boss's behavior is *that* egregious, it's probably best to report it to someone with the authority to do something about it. Or if this situation stems solely from abject incompatibility, you could inquire about other potential opportunities within your company. Even requesting a change in schedules could do the trick, if you're willing to work a different shift to get a different supervisor.

Would your partner be interested in booking a couples' massage to help you unwind? (It may not change anything at the office, but it would be a *much* more pleasant way for y'all to bond.)

Solve your short-term problems AND save your long-term relationships? Not a bad way to spend an afternoon. Not bad at all.

And per usual, nobody's perfect. If you get caught up in the moment and don't realize until midrant that you've been hogging the *Poor me* mic, you can always pause, take a breath, and switch gears. Things you could say include:

"You know what? I don't need to keep talking about this."

"Bless you for listening. I'm done now."

"It just occurred to me that I am whining at you like a Big Fucking Baby and I'm sorry. I'll stop so we can have a nice adult conversation or just sit together in companionable silence, which is also cool."

What if it's not them, it's you?

Remember the beginning of part II when we did all that good work on self-awareness and I mentioned adults who have a bad habit of lying to themselves on the reg? Right. So, when you're feeling frustrated and gearing up for a nice long whine about it, something you might wish to take into consideration is: Could the problem here…just maybe…be you? I realize it may seem like you're drowning in past-due deadlines because Demon Supervisor has been vomiting tasks on your desk like Linda Blair in *The Exorcist,* but just to play Demon Supervisor's Advocate for a moment — could it be that your workload only feels too heavy because you're, um, not very efficient at handling it? That, perhaps, if we're being toooooootally honest, you've been spending more time watching YouTube videos than cranking out your assignments, and that's why you're so behind? All I'm saying is, sometimes the world is sending you a message, and your adult job is to listen. (And maybe catch up on work this weekend instead of booking that couples' massage. Or better yet, turn it into an *incentive* for finishing your work by Friday!)

PS: Read the room

Ever found yourself bemoaning your heavy course load to the parents who sacrificed everything to send you to college? Sulking over a dating dry spell to a pal who's in the midst of a messy divorce? Complaining about your "low" annual bonus to your sister, who was recently laid off?

Ouch.

As I said at the beginning of this chapter, when you're having a hard time, you have the right to blow off steam. But also, you know, *know your audience,* and maybe save some of that shit for your journal.

Ooh, or your therapist! That's Big TFG Energy right there.

I thought I asked you not to do that

To date, I've spent hundreds of pages across multiple No Fucks Given Guides explaining how to set boundaries and stick to them. It's one of my specialties, and getting good at it will save you a lot of time, headaches, heartache, and hangovers. But in *Grow the Fuck Up,* I want to focus on the flip side of all that: **respecting *other people's* boundaries.**

Which a Total Fucking Grownup does with grace and without hesitation.

Fortunately, you've had some training on this account. Boundaries are similar to rules, like the ones your parents once laid down for "no running with scissors" or "no Candy Crush at the dinner table." Some of them were put in place to keep you safe; some were just to keep your parents sane. Some were a little bit of each.

In any case: Their house, their rules, right?

Your job was to follow those rules, or else suffer the *totally known* consequences. If you decided the punishment was worth the crime, well, that was your prerogative. (My brother was known to break a rule or four and take his grounding as the cost of doing business; I was a Goody-Two-Shoes who only missed curfew once, because I got stuck behind an accident on the only road that led to my house. But I digress.)

If you understand how rules work, you're most of the way toward being able to respect people's boundaries. The key difference is that generally speaking, **breaking one of your parents' rules had consequences that hurt YOU; whereas crossing someone else's boundary has consequences that hurt THEM.***

And I know you don't want to hurt other people. You seem nice.

Plus, **even if other people's boundaries seem silly to you, or yours to them,** we've already gone over that whole "show respect

---

* If you disrespect people's boundaries often enough, there probably *will* be consequences that hurt you. If you need to use that as additional motivation to act like a grownup here, be my guest.

and get respect back" thing. Neither of you can ascend from Theoretical Adulthood to the glittering realm of TFG-dom if you fail to honor the limits that each of you has laid out for accessing your time, energy, money, bodies, stuff, hospitality, or anything else.

Finally — and in the same way the "house rules" may have differed between your parents and your friends' parents, who let you play all the video games you wanted during mealtimes — it's important to note that **boundaries comprise a deeply personal, individual framework that will vary from person to person and relationship to relationship.** For example:

Just because one partner used to give you free rein over their iPhone does not mean that all future partners should be expected to hand over logins and passwords, no questions asked.

Just because you used to have a coworker who encouraged oversharing about your personal lives, not every future cubicle mate is going to tolerate an hour of TMI at the Xerox machine. If they beg you to dial it back because talking about your Adventures in Bumble makes them uncomfortable, then for God's sake, save your weekend hookup roundup for someone who enthusiastically consents to listen to it.

And just because YOU would tolerate a specific behavior —
say, friends stopping by your apartment unannounced at all
hours — doesn't mean everyone else would or should tolerate
it coming *from* you. If you've been asked to call first, then call
first. How easy is that?

Herewith a few more effortless ways to respect someone else's
boundaries. **All you have to do is ... NOTHING!**

BOUNDARY	HOW TO RESPECT IT
Your friend says they don't want to talk about their IVF struggles because it stresses them out.	Don't keep asking how the latest round went, no matter how supportive you think you're being.
Your date tells you they are saving themselves for marriage.	Do not push them to have sex with you tonight ... or to elope.
Your partner asks you not to bring up politics right before going to sleep, because it gives them nightmares.	Do not read AOC tweets aloud in bed, no matter how "fire" they may be.

On a final note, and as my editor wisely pointed out (Hi
Mike!) — by now you may be thinking *I totally get what you're*

saying, but what happens when someone else's boundaries conflict not with my "desires" or "preferences" but with my needs?

Like, say, the need to do your job? I gotcha. Let's discuss.

Maybe you have a boss whose expressed boundary is "Please do not send me emails. I get too many of them. If you need something from me, come by my office and ask in person."

But that boss is never *in* their office when you make the trek down the hall. Or their door is always closed. Or it's open, but when they see you hovering outside they give you the stink eye and you lose your nerve to approach. All of which is wasting your time and seriously impacting your ability to get shit done, and all of which is also drawn directly from my own experience as a twenty-two-year-old editorial assistant.

It's a pickle, but **a TFG uses their considerable critical thinking skills to come up with a solution.** I'll talk much more about being resourceful in part III, but a quick example here might be:

Call before you stop by. (Assuming there's been no moratorium placed on phone communication too . . .)

If your boss has a secretary, assistant, or shared calendar, make a formal appointment. This may require extra organization on your part, and a little more lead time, but it would be worth it to get your questions answered or permission granted so you can move forward.

If you stop by when the door is closed, leave a message with the secretary/assistant asking for a good time to come back. If there is no gatekeeper, you could try leaving a note on the door. Hey, it's not an email.

If the stink eye scares you, what did I tell you on page 53 about sucking it up, Buttercup? Knock, enter, and hope for the best. I believe in you.

> Well, it would be just plain silly of me if I didn't take this opportunity to direct you to two of my finest works on the topic of boundaries, in case you need help setting or sticking to your own. *The Life-Changing Magic of Not Giving a Fuck* is philosophical gold, and *Fuck No!* is its partner in practical application. Who's got your best interests in mind, kids? Auntie Sarah, that's who.

And that's a wrap on our **adventures in self-awareness and self-control!**

From part II, you've learned that mature adults are honest with themselves and others, and tuned in to their emotions and their privilege. They are polite and kind; their impulse control is on point; they're able to cope with and communicate their disappointment in a healthy, productive way; and they've never met a boundary they can't respect.

(And I hope you've learned a whole bunch of ways to *develop those qualities in yourself,* because otherwise Auntie Sarah is probably not getting another book contract and Uncle Judd is going to have to make peace with the pro cat lady thing.)

Now it's time to add to your slate of sophisticated adult skills, grow the fuck up, and **get RESPONSIBLE.**

Onward, to part III!

WITH GREAT RESPONSIBILITY COMES GREAT POWER:

The perks of being independent and dependable, and how to get there

Part III approaches responsible adulthood from two angles —
INDEPENDENCE (i.e., taking on responsibility) and
DEPENDABILITY (i.e., acting responsibly).

Beginning with **"If everybody else jumped off a bridge,
would you do it too?,"** we'll get you *thinking* independently
(evaluating your personal values and setting your priorities
accordingly) **so you can *act* independently** (making decisions
and following through on them). Then in **"Mommy needs a minute,"** I'll teach you how to **become more self-sufficient** by **getting
proactive and taking initiative;** followed by **"Are you sure you
looked everywhere?,"** featuring tips that'll take you from hope-
lessly helpless to **reliably resourceful.**

After that we have a couple of chapters **on wellness,** which
sits **at the crossroads of taking on responsibility AND acting
responsibly.** After all, if you can't get your own health in order,
you're not destined to be dependable to yourself or anyone else
for much of anything, are ya? Here I'll put my own spin on **"Eat
your vegetables"** (physical health) and **"Wear a helmet"** (mental
health), and then we'll move on to the back half of part III: dependability, in which **TFGs complete the tasks they set for themselves *and* the ones they've promised to deliver for others.**

A GYST-claimer

If you've read my book *Get Your Shit Together,* you'll note a few overlapping concepts in this part of *Grow the Fuck Up.* What can I say? "Having your shit together" is typically the result of "acting responsibly," and people who "are dependable" typically also "have their shit together." I don't make the rules. And also: NO SKIMMING. Repetition is how you learn.

In **"Maybe you should have thought of that before we left the house,"** I'll offer a supremely practical guide to **planning ahead, managing your time,** and **managing expectations** all around, followed by **"Do your homework,"** a paean to coming prepared. And last but not least, we'll close part III with **"Money doesn't grow on trees,"** a detour similar to the one we're taking on wellness — because in addition to tending their bodies and brains, **adults have to take responsibility for their *financial health,* too.**

Let's roll!

(Responsibly, of course.)

Independence
(taking on responsibility)

If all you ever wanted as a kid was to set your own bedtime, drink orange soda with breakfast, and categorically refuse to wear socks, then boy does adulthood sound grand. It's that magnificent, long-awaited moment when nobody can tell you what to do anymore — not your parents, not your teachers, not even the government! (Well, within reason.) You can drive and vote and smoke and drink and pair Tevas with your tux if you so choose. Who's gonna stop you? YOU'RE THE GROWNUP NOW. But while it's true that being allowed to do whatever the fuck you want is one of the great lures and rewards of this whole adulting thing, it's how you wield that newfound independence — in *thinking* for yourself and *taking action* on your own behalf — that makes or breaks your standing as a TFG. It's a big responsibility, but it's also an incredible opportunity to carve out the life you really want, and do it up right.

If everybody else jumped off a bridge, would you do it too?

I'm not so far removed from my own youth to have forgotten how going along with the crowd can feel easier and safer than going your own way. But there will be lots of times in life — not limited to your younger years — when you may not agree with "the crowd," and you'll have to get comfortable thinking and doing for yourself.

Which means you need to **get your priorities straight.**

Prioritizing is an essential life hack. There's a reason it factors prominently into all of my No Fucks Given Guides — from allocating your time, energy, and money to things and people that make you happy (*The Life-Changing Magic of Not Giving a Fuck*); to ordering the items on your to-do list based on urgency, which ensures you're getting the most necessary things done first (*Get Your Shit Together*); to dealing with things you CAN control instead of freaking out about things you CAN'T (*Calm the Fuck Down*).

But when it comes to growing the fuck up, prioritizing isn't all deadlines and to-do lists. (Though we'll get there, too, never fear!) **It's also about making choices about how you live your life based on how those choices line up with your VALUES.**

When we were kids, our life choices were heavily influenced by the values of the adults in the room. For example, if your family were dedicated churchgoers, then you probably were too. Maybe you didn't think much of it at the time, or if you did have qualms or questions about their brand of worship, maybe you didn't feel you were in a position to act on or pose them quite yet.

Or if, say, your mom felt you'd benefit more from taking piano lessons after school than playing Xbox well, the "choice" was clear, and your afternoons were full of Mozart, not Minecraft.

That kind of thing wasn't necessarily bad.* You may have been steered into some activities you wouldn't have chosen for yourself, but along the way you were **gaining essential life experience with which to form your *own* values that you could one day use as a basis for making your *own* choices** as the adult in the room. (And not for nothing, knowing how to play "Chopsticks" will forever be a good party trick.)

Independence is more than ditching church or piano lessons just because "nobody can make you go" — and it's more than rushing out to buy beer or cast a ballot just because you're finally *allowed* to. You still have to make some value-based decisions here.

---

* I mean, assuming their "church" was not actually "a dangerous cult," in which case YES ALL VERY BAD, sorry about that.

Do you *want* to use up your grocery budget on a case of White Claw? *Who* are you going to vote for, and *why*?

The choice is yours, so make it count.

Here's a little exercise for you: What do you value? It could be sleep, close friendships, leaving a legacy of kindness, being able to pay your own way, or being able to keep up physically with your grandchildren. All answers are acceptable.

WHAT DO I VALUE?

_____ _____

_____ _____

_____ _____

_____ _____

_____

How are those values reflected in your day-to-day priorities? (And if they're not, how could they be?) For example, if you really value being well rested, it makes sense to prioritize an early bedtime, or naps. If you value your close friendships, you'll want to prioritize staying in touch and letting people know you care about them. And if it turns out you value secular family fun time over organized religion, you could be taking *your* kids to the zoo or the aquarium or the ballpark on Sundays. You're in charge!

WHAT SHOULD MY DAY-TO-DAY PRIORITIES BE?

_____   _____

_____   _____

_____   _____

_____   _____

_____   _____

Now take it a step further. How can you prioritize those values with regard to grander goals and Big Life Choices? For example, Prioritizing like a Total Fucking Grownup could look like:

Choosing to enter the workforce instead of going to grad school, because you value financial security over continuing education and mounting debt. (Or vice versa.)

Choosing to start over in a new city because you value the romantic relationship that's taking you there more than you do the comfort and stability of staying put. (Or vice versa.)

Choosing to turn down a promotion that would require longer hours because you value your downtime more than professional advancement. (Or vice versa.)

And BTW, none of this is to say that your grownup values and choices should or will necessarily differ from the ones your parents modeled, or the ones "the crowd" — be they your siblings, peers, or colleagues — is going all-in on.

Only that they *might,* and if so, that's okay. **Your life is yours to live as you see fit.** And if it turns out that "what everybody else is doing" is actually pretty darn smart, interesting, fun, and good for YOU, then have at it! No need to be contrary just for the hell of it. Auntie Sarah's got that covered.

Decisions, decisions

Getting your values and priorities straight was a big first step, congratulations! But the total TFG package requires **putting your related life choices into action.**

Many Theoretical Adults will falter here, because even if they're full-on independent thinkers who know in their heart what they *want* to do — **they become paralyzed with the fear of making the "wrong" decision and never take the all-important step of, you know, DOING it.** And unfortunately, knowing what you want in life doesn't get you very far if you're too anxious or self-conscious or fearful to follow though.

If that sounds familiar, then it's time to take the bull by the horns.

Er, actually, never mind. That sounds dangerous — no wonder some people are so afraid of making the *wrong* decision that they can't make *any decision at all.* How about instead we **"anticipate the likely consequences."** Doesn't have quite the same ring to it, but far more productive than an accidental goring.

If you're worried that the decision you've independently, responsibly come to is going to turn out to be the "wrong" one, and it's keeping you from taking action, I want you to do two things:

1. Ask yourself *What's the worst that could happen?*

2. WRITE DOWN YOUR ANSWER.

I'm serious. Write it down. Things that go bump in the night are scary because you can't see them. In order to drain this decision of its paralyzing powers, you've got to blaze the lights and put it all out there, pen to paper.

And remember the key word in re: anticipating consequences: *LIKELY.* No catastrophizing, okay? (If that's your jam, I've got a whole other book you need to read.)*

---

* https://sarahknight.com/ctfd

_____

WHAT'S THE [LIKELY] WORST THAT CAN HAPPEN?

_____

_____

_____

_____

This process will help you sort out the small shit and all the way up to those grand goals and Big Life Choices. For example:

I want to wear the yellow chiffon dress for Janelle's wedding instead of the navy-blue sequined one. What's the worst that could happen?

Gee, I don't know, maybe you spend a few hours wishing you wore the blue one, but nobody else notices or cares? Is this decision worthy of haunting you to your grave? Seems unlikely.

I want to take charge and just choose the restaurant for my parents' anniversary dinner because my siblings are useless. What's the worst that could happen?

Maybe it'll suck. But if it does — and assuming you came to your decision using all of the available facts (reviews, friends' recommendations, location, parking, décor, menu, etc.) — then *anyone* might have made the same choice, right? And since *nobody else* was stepping up, you took one for the team and saved *everyone* a bunch of time and energy along the way. More mediocre cake for you!

Okay, but what if we all get food poisoning???

What did I tell you about LIKELY scenarios? Come on, I need you to focus. (And to remember the One Question to Rule Them All. Can you control for salmonella? I thought not. Carry on.)

Oh yeah, Auntie Sarah? Well, what's the worst that could happen if I choose the wrong college to attend? Or the wrong job offer to accept? Or the wrong person to spend the rest of my life with?!?!?!?

Whoa. Time out. It's true that there's a qualitative difference between wardrobe choices, menu options, and Big Life Choices, but that's the beauty of this exercise. When you think it out and write it down, you'll see that:

1. The "worst" consequences of small decisions, like choosing the yellow chiffon, are just not that bad. And certainly not worth all the mental hassle you've been putting yourself through to make this choice and act on it. Just pick a dress and have fun! (You're going to be late.)

2. And even the most reasonable worst-case scenarios for the big stuff — like choosing where to go to college — are so far off or, frankly, unknowable that it makes no sense to be granting them **more decision-making weight than what your values, your priorities, and your gut are providing you *right now*.**

Sure, choosing University of Arizona for its marketing program and ten years from now deciding you'd rather be a veterinarian and wishing you'd gone to Ohio State for their superior Animal Health offerings wouldn't be *ideal*. But is it really that bad AND that likely to happen? (And if it is, um, why are you even leaning toward U of A again? Perhaps this exercise is helping you in more ways than one, Dr. Dolittle.)

3. In any event, *nothing* **is worse than remaining mired in analysis paralysis.** Because if you never make and follow through on a decision in the first place, then you never get things like a college experience, a career, or a life partner AT ALL. Is that really how you want to play this?

Honestly, kids, you could sit here all day dreaming up the likeliest worst-case scenario for leaving your stable job to work for an exciting start-up or leaving your unfulfilling relationship to be a swingin' single, and whatever you decide, **the worst thing that happens will probably be something you never even saw coming.** That's just how life works, and even Total Fucking Grownups don't have crystal balls for brains. As long as you're sticking to your values and prioritizing your life choices accordingly, you're as good to go as you're ever gonna get.

Make up your mind, make your move, and — whatever happens — you'll live with it, learn from it, and life will go on.

More on how to manage all of that, coming right up …

Mommy needs a minute

In this chapter, we're going to work on *making* **shit happen** and, more importantly, **not** *waiting* **for other people to do it for you.**

Actual Babies are completely useless and need all the help they can get. Fine. Big Fucking Babies are useless for totally different reasons and simply *take advantage* of all the help they can get. Not fine, but I doubt they're reading, so whatever. Theoretical Adults land somewhere in the middle and you guys, I can work with. Hang tight.

Total Fucking Grownups are largely self-sufficient. They use the knowledge, power, and abilities that they possess (and, I might add, have worked maturely and responsibly to get to the *point* that they possess) to do what needs to be done. Themselves.

Like, obviously we can't send seven-year-olds to the grocery store and expect them to pick out a week's worth of healthy meals on a budget — that wouldn't be fair, because they haven't been around long enough to grasp the concepts of recipes, nutritional content, or credit card debt, among other things. But your average twenty-seven-year-old with an all-access pass to that knowledge, power, and ability I mentioned? They ought to be able to handle a Trader Joe's run. And if, instead, they still *depend* on Mom, Dad, big brother, or a very patient roommate to do it for them, that's BFB behavior, right there.

(Whereas, if they *can't* handle a task for themselves, by themselves — for whatever reason — then their responsibility lies in seeking out/arranging for alternate means of meeting their needs or achieving their goals. Delegating is a pro-dult skill we can all get on board with, and actively asking someone to do something for you is different than just waiting around and *expecting* them to.)

Now, some Theoretical Adults in the room might be thinking, *Okay, but I just never really* thought *about how much cereal and yogurt I go through in a week or how much it costs, and I totally* would *do the shopping if I had to, but it's never really been my job and I don't think that makes me a Big Fucking Baby . . . does it?*

Not necessarily! But you're still landing shy of TFG, and there's no reason you can't make the leap, what with the internet being home to more recipes than you can shake a fennel frond at, and prices and ingredients typically being printed right there on the package.

All it takes is **a bit of critical thinking on your part** — to work out your budget and dream up and streamline your menu — and you're off to the races (or in this case, the grocery store), knocking out an adult task all by your adult self. It's a beautiful thing.

PRO-DULT TIP: Back in my day, we didn't have all this newfangled technology to help run our lives smoothly; the best we could do was slap a magnetic notepad on the fridge and hope for the best. But you? You've got *options*. If you're having trouble getting organized — or really, doing anything — I assure you, there's an app for that.

And here's **the added beauty of being so gosh-darn self-sufficient:** it's not merely the necessary chores like "food acquisition" that you're able to dispatch with responsible aplomb. **Self-sufficiency is also the path toward being able to do whatever the fuck you WANT, however the fuck you want to do it** — precisely because you're no longer dependent on anybody else's version of doing it for you. For example:

If you're self-sufficient enough to get your own groceries, then you can eat whatever you want for dinner, not be dependent on the menu stylings of your roommate.

If you're self-sufficient enough to earn your own money, then you can manage it however you please, not be dependent on the goodwill (or judgment calls) of your parents or partner.

If you're self-sufficient enough to plan a vacation, then you can go wherever you like, not be dependent on the preferences of a better organized traveling companion.

Not too shabby. And there's no better place to start you down that self-sufficient path than by **being proactive** and **taking some initiative.**

Just do it. (Yourself.)

Sometimes, you'll need to take the initiative in order to **meet your own damn needs.**

> You're home alone and hungry? Come on, you can figure this out... Right! Time to make yourself a sandwich.

> You need to get a job? Update your CV and get thee to LinkedIn.

> You're out of boxer briefs? Put in a load of laundry or commit to going commando. Up to you, Tarzan.

Other times, you'll need to take the initiative in order to **get a whole group on track to collective action and success.** And while making that effort may not serve your individual, immediate needs as much as making yourself a PB&J when you're hungry, I assure you, the benefits are just around the bend.

For example, think about how many times you've been caught in a situation — say, in a classroom, at the office, or even on a family text chain — where **EVERYBODY has a problem to add to the mix, but NOBODY is offering a solution.**

"We have to figure out where we're going to fit three hundred chairs for graduation!"

"But nowhere inside is big enough! And what if it rains?"

*

"How are we going to hit this insane presentation deadline to get this client? We're stretched thin as it is!"

"We'll never make it with So-and-So already on the Such-and-Such account!"

*

"Guys, we have GOT to decide on the theme for this baby shower! We're running out of time to order party favors!"

"Ugh, I know, but Pam and Javi don't agree on anything! This is a disaster!"

Now think about HOW FUCKING FRUSTRATING that is. Right?! Fortunately, although this kind of impasse is all too common among BFBs and Theoretical Adults alike, it's also all too easy to bridge if **someone would just get up off their ass and take some initiative.**

Find the person who does that, and you've found the adultiest adult in the room. And maybe you don't think it's "fair" that in order to *be* the adultiest adult, you have to step up when nobody else will. If so, I understand where you're coming from, but I'd encourage you to **consider the benefits of YOU getting the ball rolling.**

Obviously it goes toward solving the problem, which is good for everyone. But it also **puts YOU in control of said solution,** which can be quite, shall we say, *convenient*... given that the proactive bird gets the worm AND first dibs on the least annoying part of the group project. To wit:

DOING X	GETS YOU Y
Volunteering to research the cost of a giant tent	Out of this endless meeting
Requesting an extension on a different project to free So-and-So up for this gig	Out of this endless meeting *and* a fat bonus if the big new client comes through
Telling Javi to just let Pam run point on the shower theme and there will be a nice bottle of bourbon in it for him day-of	Off this endless group chat, plus you can call "not it" on dealing with the party favors

That's **what R&R looks like when you decide to "be an adult"** in situations where everybody else is "being a bunch of useless babies." Sack up, do your chores, and at least you get to go play *eventually* instead of living out the rest of your days in a godforsaken group chat.

And in terms of **our virtuous cycle of "getting treated like an adult,"** when the useless babies (and more importantly, the TFGs in upper management) bear witness to your proactive prowess, they will see someone who is confident, capable, and dependable, and who therefore requires less coddling, coaching, and oversight.

Want to control your own destiny AND keep people off your back and out of your hair? Then taking initiative is for you!

PRO-DULT TIP: Before I was an anti-guru capable of giving zero fucks about what anybody else thinks about how I live my life, I was having difficulty asserting myself at work, and my husband said something very wise: "It's the publishing business, babe. Not the publishing friends." As an adult, you're going to have to make shit happen by [honestly, politely, respectfully] asking for what you want, pushing back against unrealistic demands, disentangling yourself from unwanted distractions, and more. If your colleagues don't like the results, they can talk shit about you to their *actual* friends over the weekend just like the rest of us.

Finally, note that **embracing a proactive mind-set is a way not only to solve existing problems, but also to create entirely *new* opportunities** for punching your TFG perks card. For example:

Just because your landlord hasn't offered you a rent reduction in exchange for you replacing the swirly orange-and-yellow 1970s kitchen tiles with ones that don't make you feel like you dropped acid in your acai bowl every morning, doesn't mean you can't *suggest* that tit-for-tat deal. Take some initiative and see what happens! (It can't be any worse than those tiles. Yowza.)

Or just because your boss hasn't noticed that one of your main competitors started gaining market share when they added more cats to their TikTok feed doesn't mean you can't point it out, accompanied by a proposal for some "strategic branding alterations" to the corporate account. You never know — you and your best friend Tuna Turner could be boopin' and floofin' your way to the corner office. *Me-ow.*

Does shooting your shot guarantee a win? Not necessarily, but **Total Fucking Grownups are willing to try AND better equipped to succeed.** If I were you, I'd take those odds.

And now, for the final entry on independent adulting, let's talk about **being resourceful.**

This is kind of a big one.

Are you sure you looked everywhere?

So...I didn't want to say this in the intro and scare you off, but humanity is on the fucking *precipice,* pals. It's a whole thing.

Between ending fascism, reversing climate change, and managing, say, at least three more worldwide plagues in the meantime, Auntie Sarah's retirement is looking mighty apocalyptic, and it's becoming increasingly clear that **we humans have a lot of work**

ahead of us to stay solvent for the next twenty-five years, let alone another six million.

COUNTERPOINT: Every time my cold, dead heart sees a news item about a teenager inventing a new method for cleaning up our oceans, **I remember that this kind of change is possible, if we can ALL learn to be more resourceful.**

Okay, well, maybe not "all" of us. I'm giving Actual Babies a pass on going the extra mile; they're busy racking up hard-earned wins like depth perception and chewing solid food. They've got enough to figure out. Nor do I begrudge a five-year-old throwing up their hands in defeat when the favorite pants that they only recently learned how to dress themselves in are nowhere to be found. Five-year-olds are not expected to understand the concepts of "looking in all of the drawers" or "checking the laundry hamper."*

But I am going to prevail on my fellow adults, Theoretical and otherwise, to **put in some more effort when it comes to finding a solution or managing a crisis.** As in:

If you can't find something, keep looking.

If you don't know how to do something, learn.

---

* Shout-out to my husband, who never met a junk drawer he could find the bottle opener in!

If you're not great at something, practice.

If something doesn't go according to plan, try a different path to get the desired result.

Or take the result you *did* get, and make do with it. Like the time there was a murder in our apartment building on Halloween weekend, and when my roommate Steve got home from work, the police wouldn't let him inside, which meant he couldn't change into his planned costume for the party we were all supposed to be going to that night.

So, he bellied up to the bar across the street and got creative. Forty-five minutes and two beers later, Steve had stripped off his button-down, borrowed a marker from the bartender, written "I went down to Georgia and all I got was this lousy T-shirt" on his undershirt, fashioned two stubby devil horns out of cardboard Stella Artois promotional coasters, and affixed them to the cowboy hat he asked his girlfriend to bring along for him on her way to the party. (Scotch tape also provided by the bartender.)

Now *that's* resourceful. Be more like Steve, everybody!*

------

*If you are too young (or perhaps too British) to get the joke, it was a riff on the Charlie Daniels Band Southern rock anthem "The Devil Went Down to Georgia." We all thought it was genius, but then, we'd also all had a few Stellas.

But seriously, **digging deeper, thinking harder, and getting creative** will serve you well in all aspects of adulting, from work to play.

If you get assigned a task — like, say, taking the minutes for the weekly management meeting — and your first instinct is *But I've never done that before, I don't know how!*, just ask whoever *used* to take the minutes to send you the last month's worth of files so you can get a feel for what it looks like.

> ### 3 questions resourceful people ask themselves on the reg
>
> Have I tried everything?
> Where can I find more info?
> What can I do with what I've got?

No need to reinvent the wheel when it's sitting right there in a Word Doc.

If you want a brand-name gadget that you can't afford, might there be a gently used one on eBay or Craigslist you could snag instead? Or a cheaper version that you'd discover is just as highly rated, if you took some time to drill down into the online reviews? Or, say you were hoping to get professional hair and makeup done before an event, but your budget won't allow; you could look into junior stylists or students as a less expensive alternative.

If you have trouble understanding the directions that came with your IKEA bedroom furniture, I'm sure there's a YouTube video that will show you how to put together the MALM or the TYSSEDAL, and you can pause it as often as necessary to mutter "Fuck!" and look around for the teeny-tiny wooden dowels you just spilled all over the floor.

If your stupid feral cat lunges at you and breaks your hand while you're on deadline and you don't have time to wait eight hours to be seen at the clinic, you could fashion yourself a splint out of two emery boards and a bandana and keep on typing. (In my defense, at the time I thought it was just a sprain. I wouldn't always advocate for at-home medical intervention in lieu of an X-ray, but it did tide me over in a pinch.)

And then you've got the whole **"saving humanity"** angle, which *slaps:*

You could be the totally resourceful TFG who figures out via online research and creativity how to turn your own little household 50 percent greener. Or if you don't have the power to get something done by yourself, you could be the neighborhood hero who organizes a block party/fundraising event to raise money for a political candidate who has the clout to take your collective values to the next level.

Your contributions don't need to be intimidatingly or prohibitively ambitious; the important thing is that **with all resourceful TFG hands on deck, they'll add up.** And when it comes to "potable water" and "livable temperatures," each of us striving for our personal grownup best sure beats the alternative.

(Although if there are any billionaire CEOs reading this, please feel free to do A LOT FUCKING MORE in re: funding alternative energy, lowering health care costs, lifting families out of poverty, shoring up our infrastructure, and maybe focusing less on "tourist travel to the moon" and more on "making the planet we have more safe, affordable, and long-term inhabitable." You know, for starters.)

Anyway, where was I?

Right, so, for one last tip for bringing out your resourceful best, we're going to take it back to our childhood roots with **a little exercise I call "Make believe and make it work."**

The next time you find yourself tempted to throw in the towel on a problem (or pawn off your responsibility on somebody else), step back for a sec and let your imagination take over. Pretend you're an intrepid explorer, a brilliant scientist, or a dogged journalist — someone who revels in making discoveries, experimenting with solutions, and pursuing leads at every opportunity.

Would Lewis and Clark let a little uncharted territory get in their way?

Would future Nobel Prize winner Dorothy Hodgkin give up on isolating the molecular structure of insulin, thus paving the way for it to be mass-produced for the treatment of diabetes, because it was "too hard"?

Would Ronan Farrow be like "Nah, guess I'll never know"?

Nope. Those Total Fucking Grownups would attack an assignment or problem with all of the resources at their disposal, and then some. I encourage you to do the same — and you can start by asking yourself the questions I provided in that helpful sidebar on page 169.

Even if you don't manage to triumph in the end (we can't all be Nobel laureates), an added bonus of having thought a little more and pushed a little harder in search of alternative solutions is that, **over time, you'll wind up amassing an arsenal of new skills that are bound to make your life easier going forward.**

Furniture building, finger splinting, emergency Halloween costumes: it's all there for you, kids!

PRO-DULT TIP: "Knowing how to change a tire" may be an archetypical example of adulting prowess, but for what it's worth, I have only been present for two tire blowouts in my entire *life*. You know what you really need to learn your way around replacing? TOILET SEATS. Mark my words, friends. Mark my words.

Moreover, in addition to helping you get shit accomplished for yourself — and potentially for the entirety of humankind — **being resourceful makes you look like a Total Fucking Grownup in the eyes of *everyone else*,** which is helpful if you want to get treated like an adult instead of like one of those annoying people who are always asking questions they could EASILY Google the answers to.

Ahem.

And now for the last bit of the first half of part III, we'll bust a couple of grownup moves in the form of **taking responsibility for your health.**

Physical AND mental.

NO SKIMMING.

Eat your vegetables

First things first, don't let the chapter title fool you. "Organizational gimmick," remember? Auntie Sarah is not here to preach the benefits of broccoli. As you might imagine, that is a discussion for a different book by a different author who has a different set of bona fides and who gives even one single fuck about potassium.

And besides, **"taking responsibility for your health" isn't all about getting your leafy greens.** That's probably some of it, but if you're looking for that kind of info you're better off getting it from a doctor, a nutritionist, or really anyone but the woman who had two bowls of Munchies Snack Mix and an Aperol Spritz for dinner last night.

(Related: I am also not here to drop weight-loss tips or police your physique. I just CANNOT with that shit.)

Instead, I'd like to share some **advice about taking care of your health that I wish *I'd* taken to heart long before my current age of forty-mumble-mumble.** And though my tips will not include the words "diet" or "exercise," I'm confident they'll contribute toward your overall well-being, which in turn will render you more energized and capable of taking all my other advice — and that's good for both of us, because you running out to tell your friends how fun and helpful I am will undoubtedly sell more books.

Hey, I know which side my cake is frosted on.

So without further ado, let's get physical with **TIP THE FIRST:**

- **There is no one-size-fits-all prescription for feelin' your best.**

Obvious? Perhaps. But given the constant onslaught of "helpful" headlines like SUGAR IS THE ENEMY and HOW TO GET THE PERFECT SUMMER BOD WITH THIS ALL-SAFFRON DIET!, I find it's *more* helpful to be reminded by a jaded old crone such as myself that not every "healthy" lifestyle choice will work or be palatable for everyone, no matter what the wellness influencers peddling superfoods, side planks, and serums on Insta would have you believe.

After forty-mumble-mumble years of fits and starts, I've learned **it's easier, more pleasant, and more effective to focus on what I *know* works for *me*.** For example:

---

5 benefits of taking responsibility for your health apart from the actual health benefits

Being able to hoist your carry-on into the overhead bin without pulling a muscle

SPF protects, but suntan lotion also makes you smell irresistible

Semiannual dental cleanings covered by insurance vs. emergency root canals that are not

Colored contact lenses are sexy!

The envy of all who gaze upon your glowing, well-hydrated skin

---

I feel like a million bucks when I manage to eat an apple once every three days. *You go, girl! Respect ya body!**

My neck and back have been hunched over a laptop writing these books for seven years straight, so for me, a massage solves more problems than a spin class.

And some days of the month, the only thing in the world my body wants is cheese, cheese, and more cheese, and I will fight anybody who tells me that I shouldn't go right ahead and eat it. OBVIOUSLY I NEED THE CALCIUM.

PRO-DULT TIP: Listen to a middle-aged woman who failed to moisturize early and often when she tells you that you should moisturize early and often. Sigh.

Now, how about YOU? **What makes you feel healthier? And while we're at it, what makes you feel like ass on a cracker?** I'm going to ask you to take a full inventory in a bit, but in case you need any, here's some inspo:

———

*™ @htmsports, IYKYK

Sleep it off

If your waking life isn't going so smoothly, perhaps there's room for improvement in Dreamland? Some people are able to conk out as soon as their heads hit their pillows and wake up feeling refreshed in five hours. Others, not so much. If the latter is more your style, engage in some **critical thinking** about the quantity and quality of your sleep, and look into things that might help you improve it.

Ideas include: earplugs, white noise, melatonin, CBD, lavender pillow spray, quitting caffeine after 3:00 p.m., or taking your TV out of the bedroom. You're also allowed to pass on your friend's "Breakfast Book Club" this Saturday because you desperately need to sleep in more than Eva needs a fifth to discuss the new Colleen Hoover. The TFG move is to put on your own oxygen — er, satin eye mask — first, before helping others.

Get it on

One thing you may *not* want to sleep on is your sexual health, my frisky friends. As a component of your overall well-being, sex might not [always] seem as imperative as eating, sleeping, and breathing, and as such, it can easily get lost in the daily grind. If that's the case — and if it's bothering you — then **reshuffle those priorities and take some initiative!**

Express your needs. Schedule sexy time with your current flame. Kindle a connection with someone new. Stock up on AAA batteries and throw yourself a party for one. Or if you're not so much looking to get it on *more* as looking for information on doing it *better* or *differently,* then it's time to **get resourceful**. To which I say: Thank God for the internet! And libraries! And inclusive local toy stores! And cool, nonjudgmental aunties who are happy to field any questions you may have!

You booze, you lose?

Far be it from Our Lady of the Aperol Spritz to critique anyone's decision to imbibe. But if you find yourself feeling groggy, foggy, and soggy too often, after too many Casamigos-soaked nights out, then you may wish to **consider the consequences** (feeling like shit, messing up at work, pissing off your friends) of your actions (ordering shots for the table... and then doing them all yourself) and **take responsibility for making changes** that will undoubtedly improve the health of your body, brain, and relationships.

Maybe go dry for a week, or get in the habit of subbing in seltzer for every other round? And don't forget the power of **incentives** to help rein yourself in — that cocktail budget you've been rocking lately could cover a sober shopping spree at Target, and Mama needs some new housewares.

PRO-DULT TIP: TAKE THE IBUPROFEN AND DRINK THE WATER *BEFORE* YOU FALL ASLEEP. Waiting till the next morning is too little, too late for your poor hardworking liver.

Okay, here's where you're taking inventory. I want you to think about the various balms and burdens on your health these days, and then write down your findings so you can start crafting helpful headlines of your own. (Remember: we'll get to mental health in the next chapter, so focus here on what makes for your best and worst *physical* self.)

I feel better when	I feel like shit when
_____	_____
_____	_____
_____	_____
_____	_____
_____	_____

Great job! The next step is to **take on the responsibility of combining the data from columns A and B** into a lifestyle that suits your body's above-expressed needs.

_But, but... it's HARD to _____ and _____ (and not _____)!_

Yes, well, adulting can be hard, Snookums. We've been over that. We've also been over "ways to make it easier" — including **getting into some good habits** (An apple every three days? COME AT ME, FIBER!); and "ways to make it more pleasant" — such as **incentivizing yourself.** Maybe you get to go to a movie this weekend if you remember to drink eight glasses of water every day this week? (Just go easy on the liquids before showtime; you don't want to waste your reward taking three trips to the Cineplex restroom.)

Ew, gross!

Real talk: as an adult, you're going to have to confront some uncomfortable truths — like, physically uncomfortable ones — such as UTIs, yeast infections, hemorrhoids, and all manner of gnarly stuff that nobody *wants to* deal with, but most of us *have to,* at one point or another. The sooner you take responsibility for these grownup gross-outs, the better. I know it was less embarrassing back when your mom was buying your butt cream, but believe me, posting up at the CVS checkout with a tube of Preparation H is much more pleasant than letting things get out of control on the bum front.

PS: In my experience, a child-sized inner-tube floatie is just as good as a 'roid donut, and the checkout clerk will be none the wiser. You're welcome.

Once you get a handle on your highly personalized prescription for feelin' fine, give it up for **TIP THE SECOND!**

- **Ignore the noise.**

Don't let yourself get sidetracked or self-care-shamed by anyone else's ideas about what works for *them* and which they therefore think *should* work for *you.* As mentioned, independent TFGs have to think and fend for themselves in all sorts of ways — including rejecting pressure to conform to other people's notions and standards when it's their own health on the line. For example:

You may find yourself in the unenviable position of being allergic to or adversely affected by "healthy" or "normal" foods, and you may be surprised at how many people either don't understand what's going on with you or don't believe you, and keep saying, "Come on, one piece of cheesecake can't hurt!" Fuck those people. If you know in your gut that gluten or dairy messes with your system, then don't let yourself get goaded or gaslit into consuming it.

You may have battled eating disorders in the past, and no matter how much your friends swear by intermittent fasting, you know in your heart that restriction is not any healthier for YOU than overindulgence. You're allowed to find your happy medium (for me, it's "everything in moderation," including Munchies Snack Mix) and live there rent-free, the 16/8 method and the 5:2 diet be damned.

You may be totally committed to the cult of CrossFit. Good for you, and I hope you'll feel comfortable standing firm in your personal wellness regimen even if *some* people see fit to snark on your sweat-soaked methods.*

---

* It me. I have been known to snark on CrossFit.

PRO-DULT TIP: Playing house is all fun and games until somebody breaks a glass in the sink or takes a cheese grater to the knuckles. You'd do well to keep your adult lair stocked with simple first aid accoutrements — or at least associate with/live downstairs from people who do — a lesson my friend Liz learned the day she called up to inquire, "Do you guys have any *really big* Band-Aids?" Yes, yes we did.

As for my final piece of advice for maintaining your physical health, I acknowledge the privilege inherent in both *giving it* and *being able to take it*, but with that said, I am a big believer in **TIP THE THIRD,** a two-parter:

- **Get yourself a doctor.**
- **And then actually go see them. Like, regularly.**

Health care in the United States is bonkers batshit apocalyptic.*
The system, she is broken — and expensive, whether or not you have insurance. As such, I understand that "getting a doctor" can be a tall order. (Let alone keeping one! I just found out that my OB/GYN of twenty years no longer takes my insurance, so looks

---

* And probably most places where this book is being published, except Canada and the Nordics. Love you guys!

like I'll be adulting my way toward finding a new person I trust to spelunk my nethers in 2023.)

Plus, not all doctors are good — some of them have a terrible bedside manner and/or inexcusable biases against women, POC, or queer, fat, or disabled patients.

Additionally and as per Tip the Third, Part Two, *"going to* the doctor" can be prohibitively challenging if you can't get paid time off work to do so, or if you have to travel long-distance because your community is underserved on the medical care front.

ALL OF THIS IS TRUE.

But for the sake of argument, let's say you DO have the time, energy, money, and gumption it takes both to get a doctor and to go see them. That's terrific! Now…when was the last time you did it?

Uh huh.

Trust me, I understand that **making the effort to make that appointment doesn't always seem important,** especially when you're twenty-one or twenty-five or even thirty-two. But then — and trust me here, too — one day your entire body will decide to fall apart cell by cell and boy would it be great if you had a professional to help you navigate that shit.

Why suffer through daily mystery headaches that turn out to be treatable allergies? Or persistent back pain that a chiropractor was put on this earth to alleviate for you?

Not to mention the preventable or early-detectable stuff that having a doctor can seriously help you, um, prevent and/or detect early. Perhaps, like me, you recently woke up in a panic in the middle of the night realizing that your mother was EXACTLY YOUR AGE when she had a heart attack, and oh also only ten years older than you are now when she was diagnosed with breast cancer, so it'd probably be a good idea to start monitoring your lipids and lymph nodes and whatnot with the aid of an aforementioned professional.

And if nothing else, why drive yourself crazy with worry when just going in for a checkup could provide valuable peace of mind about that round, itchy rash whose symptoms you would otherwise plug into WebMD at 2:00 a.m. and construe as certain death? (It's probably just ringworm, which isn't nearly as bad as it sounds. Get some antifungal cream on there and you'll be wearing short sleeves in a week.)

Anyway, as I said, getting a/going to the doctor may be a tall order. Perhaps too tall. **But if you DO HAVE the means and opportunity, then for the love of all that is treatable, preventable, and early-detectable: I urge you to summon the gumption and USE IT.**

And while you're on this kick, remember that **wellness isn't only for your skin and bones; it's for your big beautiful brain too.**

Wear a helmet*

Mental health is just as important as physical health. But due to factors like stigma, shame, and a general lack of awareness *of* its importance and *what* can be done to promote it — very **few of us show up to adulthood armed with the information we need to be able to take care of our brains the way we take care of our bods.**

And I gotta tell you, I was not remotely prepared for the worst my big, beautiful brain would have to offer — from the day I passed out in my Midtown Manhattan office building from Baby's First Panic Attack (at age thirty-ish) through the subsequent battles with anxiety and depression that cast a pall over the next decade, and which I'm still working through every damn day.

All of that is why I've always tried to use my books and my platform to shout about mental health. I won't claim to be an expert in

---

* Get it? To protect your head! (I don't know about you, but *I'm* having fun over here.)

diagnosis or treatment, but when it comes to reducing stigma and raising awareness?

For better or worse, that I feel more than qualified to do.

Go Pro

This seems like a good time to clearly state that your favorite auntie-guru is neither a doctor nor a licensed therapist. And furthermore, although I've counseled in these pages that "adulting means sucking it up and doing stuff even when it's hard" — if it's merely getting out of bed or getting out of the house that's starting to get really hard for you, that's probably not BFB-ing so much as it might be "experiencing a severe mental health issue that needs addressing." In which case, calling in the professionals is your best course of action, and I encourage you to do so. They probably won't say "fuck" as much as I do, but you can't win 'em all.

Disclaimer thus disclaimed, here are a few things I hope you'll keep in mind about **taking responsibility for your own big, beautiful brain:**

- **You needn't already be "in the weeds" to reap the benefits of mental health care.**

Anyone can see a therapist, or look into simpler (and cheaper) ways to help themselves recenter and destress — like taking up gardening or journaling; playing the Wordle or doing crossword puzzles daily; or going on long walks or giving yoga a try, which could be a bonus boon for your physical health too. And in fact, by engaging in a few **proactive prophylactic measures,** you might be doing yourself the gigantic fucking favor of never getting into the weeds at all. Self-care: it's the ultimate responsible act!

- **If you're past the point of *preventative* care, there are plenty of strategies, medical and otherwise, for managing your symptoms and feeling much, MUCH better. Here's my best [nonprofessional] advice on getting started:**

Run, don't walk

When you notice you're having a hard time, don't *waste* time waiting to deal with it. You have a responsibility to yourself to acknowledge what's happening, and act on it. I speak from agonizingly drawn-out experience here, having waited way too long to get my mental health in order after the need was made abundantly clear. I put it off because I was too busy; it wasn't that bad; okay, it *was* that bad but I was still too busy; I wasn't ready to admit I needed help; I worried that being less anxious would somehow make me lose my ambitious edge. (Spoiler: it didn't.) And on and on. The delay between realizing I needed help and actually seeking it out resulted in years of unnecessary misery — YEARS — for me, my husband, my family, and probably no small number of my coworkers.

Whether you're fifteen or fifty-five, your mental health is too important to ignore, so grow the fuck up and get on it! But also —

Don't beat yourself up

It may take a few false starts before you find what works for you, and because brains are mysterious and fickle, it might not *always* work, and sometimes it'll *stop* working and you'll have to try something new. I've been faithfully taking my Zoloft every day for a decade and I finally had to try *meditating* to get me through the Cursed Summer of 2020. Truly never thought I'd see the day, folks. (Even more surprising? IT HELPED.)

Taking initiative and resourcefully seeking solutions are the big, responsible wins here — the only other thing you owe yourself is compassion while you keep at it.

But do *listen* up

One of the biggest problems with maintaining your mental health is that you may not always know there IS a problem. You might feel stressed out, agitated, low-energy, or otherwise in a funk, but you might not realize quite how far gone you are, and that is often precisely *because* you are so far gone. Mental illness is funny like that.

If there comes a point when someone you trust and who knows you well suggests that you seem to be experiencing an unusual level of distress, it's probably a good idea to take them at their word, and revert to the previous two tips. (Especially if more than one someone suggests that…more than once.) I promise that most people don't go around accusing their loved ones of being mentally unstable for shits and giggles; they just want you to feel better. And so do I.

- **And whatever stage you're in with regard to the care and feeding of your mental health, please know that there is no reason at all to be ashamed of doing so.**

I can't reach in there and flip a switch in your brain that disappears those feelings. I wish I could! But at least I can join the chorus of voices *outside* your head that are telling you it's normal and smart and necessary to make mental health care a priority. You deserve it.

I'm sure it's obvious from everything I've said here that there's a lot of **RELIEF** to be found in addressing any mental health problem, be it a stressful week, a bout of burnout, or a lifelong struggle with depression. And for many of us, that's more than enough GTFU MO-tivation to get going. But there are a lot of **REWARDS,** too — true bright spots that you can look forward to basking in when you put your mental house in order.

Your relationships may improve. Your energy levels may increase. You may gain (or regain) confidence. You may find new inspiration and motivation, and be able to access more joy. You may even feel so good and newly energetic, confident, and inspired that you quit your job and move to the tropics and write a bestselling book about not giving a fuck.

Hey, it's been known to happen.

Dependability
(acting responsibly)

Total Fucking Grownups are independent thinkers who take responsibility for their own shit, but they can ALSO be trusted to do what they said they were going to do, when they said they were going to do it, *for other people*. And if for some reason they can't fulfill an obligation as promised and on schedule, they'll be sure to let you know in advance. How cool is that! They accomplish all of this by planning ahead, doing their homework, and managing expectations as wisely as they manage their time — aka taking responsible action that lands them in the TFG sweet spot of both being an adult and getting treated like one. Because let me tell you: nobody likes, respects, or trusts anybody more than SOMEONE THEY KNOW THEY CAN DEPEND ON.

Maybe you should have thought of that before we left the house

The path toward becoming a Totally Fucking Dependable Total Fucking Grownup begins with you **thinking things through.**

Per usual, Actual Babies can't do this and Big Fucking Babies won't, but Theoretical Adults may not always realize they *should*. They're not necessarily inept or lazy, but they do say things like "Haha, I'm not much of a planner!" and even if they do manage to get shit taken care of, it's not without a bunch of last-minute chaos that gives themselves and everyone else a shit-ton of unnecessary agita along the way.

I know you can do better. **You can make your life — and everyone else's — easier and more pleasant with a bit more advance planning.**

PRO-DULT TIP: Don't start the job until you have all the materials on hand and in working order. To be honest, it's taken me a few deeply annoying tries to learn this lesson, one of which involved the absence of a rather important kitchen appliance for a rather extensive period of time. And it goes for all kinds of projects, from baking a pie to painting a room to building out that DIY "EasyCloset" system you ordered. The worst time to find out you need a hacksaw that you don't own is at 9:00 p.m. on a Sunday night without an open Home Depot in sight.

Ugh, I already have to do this thing, and now you're saying I have to think about HOW I'm going to do it? I can't just get going and hope for the best??

In a word, no. In ninety-five words: Nobody's asking you to go out and buy a bullet journal to document your every step of every hour of every day. That sounds both annoying and inefficient, two things I would never endorse. But if you run out of options or time because you didn't take a beat to look at the big picture before you got started, that's *even more annoying* and *even less efficient*. And unfortunately, your best intentions count for bupkis when you were never going to be able to follow through on them due to your own lack of foresight.

For example, if you promised your elderly neighbor you'd do her raking this weekend, you should check the weather forecast. This way if it looks like rain on Sunday, you'll know to get out there and git 'er done on Saturday before the skies open up and Mrs. Petrillo's lawn becomes a soggy, mulchy wasteland.

Or if you're *about to promise* your coworker that you can cover their late shift on Saturday, you should first take your raking duties into consideration (AND check the weather). And then if Sunday is indeed looking drizzly, decide whether it's a good idea for you to be on your feet behind the bar for eight hours after you spent all day Saturday dragging Mrs. P's back forty.

In all of the above scenarios, the idea is to [critically] think it through, so you don't set anybody up for disappointment (or set yourself up for back spasms.) In other words: **anticipate** [the potential consequences] so you can **orchestrate** [a dependable outcome].

Huh. Where have I heard that before?

With all this in mind, here are three tips to get you started on **becoming a Totally Fucking Dependable Total Fucking Grownup.** A TFD TFG, if you will.

Don't overcommit

Did you know that it's a lot easier to do what you said you were going to do if what you said you were going to do is eminently manageable in the first place? #TRUTH. Take on less, so you can deliver more dependably overall. Like, if you're not sure you'll have time to stop at the grocery store in the next two days, DON'T OFFER TO BRING THE PAPER PLATES TO THE PICNIC, DUMMY. Instead, raise your hand for cleanup duty; since you're already going to be there, you can't fuck this up. Your gold star awaits.

BONUS: Undercommitting means you've got more opportunity to *over*deliver. (Surprise! Look who brought pot brownies!) Not strictly necessary for top-of-the-line adulting, but still a neat trick.

Spell it out (*set* expectations)

I cannot emphasize enough how positively adult*eriffic* it is to TELL PEOPLE WHAT THEY CAN EXPECT FROM YOU. From the get-go. There is no need to cultivate an air of mystery here. Mysterious people are not dependable. Wishy-washy, noncommittal people are not dependable. Actual Babies = utterly dependent, not at all dependable. You get the drift.

As for the tasks you've [ideally under-]committed to — and as I've advised re: all adult communications — now be honest, polite, and straightforward about how and when you plan to accomplish them. It's for your own good. Just as becoming self-sufficient lets you live and work in peace, vocalizing your intentions means people don't have to guess and hope and wonder and eventually poke and prod and annoy the everloving shit out of you before you're good and ready to deliver. They'll know exactly when to expect your half of the rent, your notes on the sales meeting, your thoughts on which flowers go best with the bridesmaid dresses, and all the rest...because you already told them. Fancy that!

And the more often you deliver on exactly what you told people to expect — which should be that much easier to do since you set those expectations your own adult self — the more your reputation as a TFD TFG grows, and the more leeway you'll earn for the times you really need it. In which case...

Rein it in (*manage* expectations)
If and when you realize that your shit's going sideways, then do everyone the favor of telling them what's going on and what you're *now* capable (or not capable) of delivering under these revised circumstances.

A-S-A-F-P.

If you need more time to get the cash together, say so. If you spent last night in the ER and need an extension, say so. If your own in-laws surprised you with a visit this weekend and you have to reschedule the Bouquet Summit for

Monday night, JUST. SAY. SO. Hello, communication skills! **The only thing worse than a person you can't depend on is one who totally could've given you a heads-up, and didn't.**

And BTW, you're well within your rights to shift things around because you *want to,* not just because an ill-timed ice storm or bout of gastroenteritis *forced you to.* But in such cases, it's *even more important* to manage people's expectations as early and honestly as you can, since you have no act of God or bad shawarma on which to blame your bailout.

Friends notice when you last-minute cancel on that standing Wednesday dinner plan five weeks in a row, and they also notice that you never miss a weekday spin class (they see it all over your Reels). So instead of making them feel like you don't care enough to get together or that you're too fucking flighty to bother making plans with at all, just say, "I really want to see you guys, but work is out of control right now and spin is the only thing keeping me sane, so weeknight dinners are probably not in the cards."

And then maybe set some new expectations around "Sunday brunch."

PRO-DULT TIP: This one's more get-your-shit-together than grow-the-fuck-up, but it's my book, and I am an EVANGELIST for packing cubes. If you want to travel around Europe for three weeks with a single carry-on *and* be able to easily plunk your stuff into a drawer and pluck it back out again every time you change hotels, those li'l zippered wizards are your new best friends.

So those were some general tips for getting your dependable engine running. Now let's dive a little deeper in the only way your Type-A Auntie knows how: by **making a plan.**

And look, I'm not saying you have to take it to extremes. Not all of us pack three days before a trip <cough> or do our holiday shopping in July, nor do we need to become those people. **Flying blind, however, is the *other* extreme — and therein lies a Theoretical-Adult-bordering-on-BFB.**

And the reality is, when you completely eschew thinking things through ahead of time, you're likely to wind up struggling to figure shit out midtask, making a few woulda-been-avoidable missteps in the process, and then wasting even more time on corrective action. All of which means **you are probably NOT, in fact, going to be able to do what you said you were going to do, when you said you were going to do it,** plus you'll have proven yourself undependable to other people and made everything that much harder on *yourself* while you were at it.

Why in Beyoncé's name would you want to do that? **Instead, just think ahead!**

To that end, I've got **THREE MORE TRUSTY TIPS** to help you go from "Haha, I'm not much of a planner!" to "No worries, I'm on it!"

'Twas the night before I had shit to do

Run through tomorrow's game plan tonight — easy enough to do while you're brushing your teeth, or taking the dog for his evening poo.

For example, if you told your friend you would come over at noon on Saturday to help them study for their real estate license (and that you'd pick up emotional support bagels on your way), use Friday evening to give advance consideration to things like "traffic" and "bus schedules" and "people who didn't fucking make up their mind before they got to the counter." It's much easier and more pleasant to identify potential variables and plan/account for them *beforehand* than it is to be tapping out a "sorry, running late" text while balancing two hot coffees, a half dozen cinnamon raisin, and a tub of cream cheese on your lap in the back of an emergency Uber.

Take the long view

Now, consider your whole week. Are there certain days you could more easily devote to certain tasks or activities? Like, if you know Mondays and Tuesdays are always your busiest at work, you could try to keep Wednesdays lightly scheduled to allow for midweek "catch-up." This way you'll be better situated to handle any Monday/Tuesday overflow, which in turn reduces your chances of falling so far behind that you completely blow (or have to bail on) a work or social commitment later in the week.

You can even look at the entire month and decide that every other Tuesday night is for laundry. That'll keep you in clean socks, AND help dependably free up your weekends for something more fun than *folding* socks.

Heck, have you heard of a five-year plan? There are no limits on thinking ahead, friends!

Put it in writing

Now imagine you're facing a complicated and consequential task, like relocating to a new city or redesigning your company's website. Successful execution is going to require more than having taken a quick mental inventory while Pawbert DeNiro did his business last night, or even having the benefit of a slow Wednesday to sort your shit out.

Now is the time to go full adult and **MAKE A FUCKING LIST.** Your auntie Sarah, she loves a list.

If you spend half an hour thinking through and writing down all the steps you'll need to take in order to complete your complicated, consequential task, I promise you will not regret it. You're also less likely to miss a step (or three), which would necessitate a lot more than half an hour of last-minute stress and full-body hives in the long run.

Plus, seeing everything laid out on the page makes it easier to map out the correct order of operations, so you won't wind up putting down a nonrefundable deposit with

U-Haul *before* you find out your new apartment building doesn't allow move-ins on Mondays, or promising your boss an unrealistic go-live date that doesn't take into account the two nonnegotiable weeks off your head programmer is taking for their honeymoon.

Make. A. List.

And kids? If any of this is starting to sound onerous, allow me to remind you that just like every single piece of advice in this entire book, **becoming totally fucking dependable benefits YOU as much as it benefits anybody else.**

Among other things, TFD TFGs get rewarded with all that freedom, autonomy, respect, and trust I mentioned earlier (lolz); while everyone else gets hounded by clients, passed over for promotions, and quietly excluded from plans that require friends who can be depended on to show up with the paper plates THEY VOLUNTEERED TO BRING to the picnic.

Actions and behavior, they have consequences! Who knew?

Anyhoo, by now I trust you're well equipped to do what you said you would do. Which means it's time for a brief tutorial in **honing your time management skills — aka the "when you said you would do it" part.**

Everything is going to take longer and cost more than *everybody* tells you it will. From recipes to renovations, you'd do well to plan for overages.

Find your shoes, it's time to go!

Barring unforeseen circumstances — under which, as noted, they would be adept at resetting expectations — Total Fucking Grown-ups can be counted on to meet deadlines on projects, applications, and fantasy football rosters, and to arrive on time for dinner without their friends having to send passive-aggressive reminder texts at fifteen-minute intervals in the five hours leading up to the res.

And all of that is swell, but it's also…not hard to accomplish. Sure, some BFBs are late because they don't respect people or processes, but **plenty of fuckos with otherwise immature and irresponsible inclinations can still manage to be on time.***

So why doesn't everybody do it? Why are there so many Theoretical Adults out there for whom TFG-dom would be reliably in reach if they could just stop believing that "I don't know, I'm just a late person!" was an acceptable excuse for being perennially twenty minutes past due?

---

* Seriously. I'm making a mental list of such people right now, and it's kind of blowing my mind.

It's not acceptable. And it's a hill your auntie Sarah will die on, because being on time isn't some kind of superpower. It's perfectly easy to do, and it **starts with knowing the answer to a very simple question:**

How long is this gonna take?

i.e., to get somewhere —

There's a party at Rico's this weekend, and it's a surprise for his boyfriend's thirtieth, so everyone really needs to be assembled in advance of the guest of honor's arrival.

Lucky for you, with Google Maps in this world, there's no excuse for thinking it takes ten minutes to get to their place when it most certainly takes twenty. (Thirty, in rush-hour traffic.) Look at your driving, walking, or public transport routes beforehand. If your city has an app that broadcasts subway and train delays, use it. If you know you have to pick up Daisy on your way and *she's* always late, factor in fifteen minutes of waiting for her to find her shoes. (And tell her she better hurry, or she'll have to find another ride too.)

i.e., to do something —

Have you been asked to read your classmate's 400-page novel in time to show up for a critique session on Monday? Do you, um, know how long it takes you to read 400 pages? If not, then I suggest you time yourself reading the first 20 so you can extrapolate before you commit to that Monday meet-up.

The same goes for knowing how long it takes you to shower and shave, or to blow-dry your hair. If you're not sure, then just clock yourself doing those things for a week, write down the data, note the pattern, and stop promising your sister you'll "be there in ten" when it is clearly going to take you "forty-five."

See? I told you this was easy. When you know how long it takes to get places and do things, you can **PLAN ACCORDINGLY** — two pro-dult maneuvers for the price of one!

And if the duration of your planned activities is out of your control and therefore unknowable — as with doctor appointments, haircuts, or sale-shopping with your mother-in-law — then please reference the very first tip from this whole motherfucking chapter: **DON'T OVERCOMMIT, and don't plan to do *other*** *things* **back-to-back.** Your boss isn't going to take "stuck in the Saks Casuals Department" as an excuse for missing that marketing meeting.

PRO-DULT TIP: Now that you're responsible for booking your own haircuts, physical therapy, and hard-to-get dinner reservations, keep in mind that you are a mere cog in a massive scheduling ecosystem that doesn't care that you "need to get in tomorrow." A little extra lead time never hurt anybody. (And definitely don't wait for the day before your brow specialist goes on maternity leave to call about getting a touch-up. She'll be with you in four to six months.)

Planning is cool, but have you tried execution?

This brings us to another time management skill: **prioritizing** — not the "making choices based on your values" kind that we discussed earlier; just the standard "getting on task and staying there" kind. Told ya we'd get here eventually. And since the Bible on this topic has already been written, I see no reason not to cite it chapter and verse.

Behold, one of my most popular tools from *Get Your Shit Together,* the Must-Do Method:

THE MUST-DO METHOD

1. MAKE A TO-DO LIST.

2. PRIORITIZE ITEMS BASED ON URGENCY.

3. MOVE WHAT HAS TO GET DONE <u>TODAY</u> TO A MUST-DO LIST.

4. DO THAT STUFF AND SAVE THE REST FOR TOMORROW.

5. REPEAT STEPS 1-4.

The MDM is gold for any Theoretical Adult who, again, is not so much a lazy BFB, but may be overwhelmed by their to-do list and/or doesn't know where to begin. **Prioritizing by urgency takes the guesswork (and a lot of the anxiety) right out of it.**

Anyway, I originally designed this method to help people *get* on task, but it occurs to me now that with a wee adjustment, it would be equally useful for the kind of **midway remobilizing you may need to do to *stay* on task.** Because even the best-laid plans will get the hiccups, and a Total Fucking Grownup knows how to pivot.

Let's look at the **MDM 2.0** in action:

THE MDM 2.0

FOR STAYING ON TASK WHEN SHIT GOES SIDEWAYS

1. LOOK AT YOUR MUST-DO LIST.
2. RE-PRIORITIZE ITEMS BASED ON URGENCY.
3. MOVE WHAT NOW HAS TO GET DONE TODAY TO THE TOP OF THE LIST.
4. DO THAT STUFF AND RE-SET/MANAGE EXPECTATIONS FOR THE REST.
5. REPEAT STEPS 1-4.

Say you work at a print shop, and you promised to have the Joplin Jackrabbits tee ball uniforms ready for pickup by Coach Malone on Monday morning. You planned ahead and gave yourself enough time to get it done. In fact, everything was packed and stacked on Friday before you left work…but never in a million years could you have *anticipated* the burst pipe over the weekend that resulted in all the jerseys getting soaked, along with the beginnings of the Barbara's Bachelorette custom tank top order you were on track to deliver on Wednesday. *Fuuuuuck.*

So now you've got a flood to clean up and two clients depending on you in the near term, one of whom is going to walk through the door any minute. Coach's kids need their uniforms to face the Moberly Mountain Lions tomorrow afternoon (a fearsome squad), and right now, their shirts are mildewing in your stockroom.

If you want to send Coach away happy and keep your Yelp rating intact, **you're going to have to [re]prioritize.**

Looks like Monday's task just went from "leisurely putting the finishing touches on the bachelorette tank tops" to "washing/drying/pressing eighteen unis that *you'll* deliver to the Jackrabbits' clubhouse first thing on Tuesday." (While the jerseys are in the dryer, you can tackle the puddles on the floor, toss any unsalvageable materials, and make a shopping list for new inventory.)

And although all of that will take a big chunk out of the time you'd so responsibly set aside to get Babs's tank top order finished, it's still doable if you reschedule a call with that ink vendor you were considering switching to (low priority), and cancel Taco Tuesday lunch with your buddy Glenn (not a priority at all).

There, glad that's sorted! And what have we learned?

If planning ahead and understanding how time works help you get organized, **prioritizing helps you *stay* organized.** And all of it makes you the TFD TFG in situations that would send your Theoretical Adult brethren crying into their tacos. Well played.

But there is one more thing…

Do your homework

Homework used to entail sitting in your room studying for a test, heading to the library to research a term paper, or forcing your sister to listen to you rehearse your oral report on *The Great Gatsby* while she was in the shower. And there was a fairly narrow range of outcomes: if you did well on the assignment, great, you got credit and moved on with your life; and if you *didn't* do well, the only person it affected was you (i.e., your grades, and your likelihood of getting grounded for said grades).

But as an adult, you're going to have to study, research, and rehearse lots more shit — and **lots more people will be depending on you to show up prepared.** It's a big responsibility, and one that Total Fucking Grownups take seriously, in part because they sure do appreciate it when other people do the same.

For example, remember how *you* were depending on your buddy Randy to organize the hotel on your last friend-cation, and everything went tits up because the Ran Man just dragged everybody to the first place he Googled without having read any of the *savage* reviews that would have warned you to steer well clear of that one-star hellhole?

Yeah. Don't be like Randy.

A Big Fucking Baby ignores facts and cuts corners to their own

> **5 ways to do your homework**
>
> Read the fine print
> Call ahead with questions
> Learn the names of the
>   people who'll be at the
>   meeting
> Practice your lines
> Find out *beforehand*
>   whether the place is
>   cash-only

and everyone else's detriment. A Theoretical Adult is more responsible overall, but also more likely to be satisfied with half measures. Which is all well and good if you're just trying to muddle through tenth-grade American lit with a vague understanding of Nick Carraway & Co., but that shit doesn't fly when other people's performance, comfort, or needs are on the line.

Instead, just **buckle down, do your homework, and come prepared.** Be the TFG who does their part and does it well, whether it's finding the hotel with the best group rate (AND REVIEWS, RANDY) for next year's friend-cation, or finding a conference room in your office building that will impress potential clients with its reliable Wi-Fi, comfortable chairs, *and* killer view. You — and everyone else — will be better off for it.

And frankly, even when they're on a solo mission, a Total Fucking Grownup knows it **makes their *own* life significantly better to trade a little more front-end prep for the best back-end results**.

I mean, if you're going to bother taking on an adult responsibility like, for example, buying a new air conditioner, why *wouldn't* you do your due diligence to ensure you're getting the best one for the price you can afford? Putting in the effort now results in not only a more pleasant summer sleeping situation, but also the likelihood that your Big Adult Purchase will last longer and work better than if you'd just showed up at Best Buy with a blindfold and a dart.

(Which you probably shouldn't do for a variety of reasons.)

I used to poke fun at my dad's devotion to *Consumer Reports,* but you better believe that anytime the man had to buy a car, a TV, or a lawn mower, he'd pored over all the relevant facts, figures, and reviews and was **making an informed decision that would reward him with the most reliable exchange of cash for goods.**

These days you can just "go online to the Wirecutter" rather than "hoard stacks of print mag back issues just in case they might come in handy," but same idea.

Oh, and while you're at it, don't forget to compare warranties! A favorable one could save you money and a lot of hassle down the line, and that's a two-for-one deal on reward *and* relief.

And one last word on all that stuff you did your homework to acquire — when you have nice things that you bought and paid for yourself, the responsibility also falls to you to *keep* them nice.

Ways to grow up and glow up include: perform regular maintenance on things like cars, guitars, and the aforementioned AC units; clean your jewelry; rotate your sofa cushions; and instead of sacrificing to buy new ones, first try getting your favorite shoes resoled. With three $20 trips to the cobbler, I got an extra ten years out of the only pair of black leather boots that have ever zipped over my calves. *Score.*

PRO-DULT TIP: Give some thought to the proximity of likely sale weekends. If you're willing to suffer a few stuffy nights in June, then biding your time on that AC unit and striking while the Fourth of July 40-percent-off discount code is hot is a Total Adult Move.

Alright, kiddo, we are movin' and we are shakin'. There's just one more order of responsible business here in part III, and that's **MONEY, HONEY.**

If you just got a little extra anxious about broaching that subject, you're not alone. Your relationship to the Almighty Dollar/Pound/Euro/Ruble/Etc. can sometimes be as icky to talk about as hemorrhoids and tricky to deal with as balancing your brain chemistry, but the good news is: **everything you really need to know about maintaining your *financial* health?**

You've already learned it.

Money doesn't grow on trees

One thing my survey respondents of all ages agreed upon was that they felt **woefully unprepared to "deal with money stuff"**

in adulthood. This makes total sense, given that making a decent living is hard, as is saving for retirement (aka the years when you would love to not *have to* be out there making a living anymore), as is juggling "the bare necessities" with "the steepest rent increases of the modern era."

Oh, plus the fact that **capitalism is the scourge of the earth.**

Unfortunately, there's not much I can do about any of that, which is part of the reason Auntie Sarah put this off until the end of part III.

But also, I confess that the idea of giving out money tips makes me feel weird. I'm no economist (nor particularly good at math, tbh), and I only have my own experience to draw from, which is essentially "middle-class-meets-upward-trajectory-powered-by-access-to-higher-education-among-other-things." And I know that not everyone has a solid support network and not everybody is granted the same opportunities I was, for reasons ranging from generational poverty to systemic racism to bad luck, and more, so I'm wary of becoming the poster auntie for out-of-touch elites whose cumulative privilege and boundless access to avocado toast have thus far shielded them from the worst financial calamities life has to offer.

That said, it would also be awfully *irresponsible* of me to skip over a rather essential element of adulting just because it makes me sweat my privilege, eh?

So what I'd like to do here — rather than hand out stock tips or act like I have any idea what an interest rate is — is to show you how "dealing with money stuff" **relies on the same skills and qualities we've already discussed** in re: "dealing with" the rest of your grownup life. For example:

Critical thinking? *Check.*

Prioritizing? *Check.*

Resourcefulness? *TRIPLE CHECK.*

If you can focus on applying these and other adult actions and behavior to bolster the ups and weather the downs of your financial life, then **no matter how much raw material you have to work with, you know you'll be doing the best you CAN with whatever you've GOT.** And that's TFG all the way.

Let's start with **BUDGETING,** a basic grownup go-to.

When I was ten, my parents started giving me a small allowance. They were both public school teachers, so we weren't rolling in it; I'm talking like two dollars a week, with a "raise" each year. It was up to me to either spend it as it came in on Garbage Pail Kids and neon hair scrunchies, or save up a couple months' worth for the latest Baby-Sitters Club book or a trendy Vuarnet T-shirt.

The key word here being "or." I would have to ask myself things like —

How much do X, Y, and Z cost, vs. how much I have to spend?

Which one do I want the most?

Do I really need another scrunchie?

Et voilà! Critical thinking and prioritizing, in effect.

Of course, at the time I was a middle schooler whose basic needs were still being met by my parents — it's not like I was choosing between hair ties and rent, or groceries. But thanks to their willingness and ability to give me an early education in financial independence, I was able to take that youthful experience in budgeting forward into my adult life and use it when I *was* responsible for my own needs and *did* have to pay for my own Kraft Mac & Cheese. And I still use it today, even though my needs and means have changed a lot over time.

The thing is, whatever its size or confines might be, a budget is a budget. It's all these adult strategies I've been preaching that will help you set and stick to it — and if need be, find creative ways to work as well as you can around it.

On that note, if you're in the difficult position of having to stretch your income to the very last dollar on the very last day of the month, **prioritizing is your friend.** And sometimes it can get a little hairy, but we do what we gotta do. When I moved to New York in my twenties, in order to keep *most* of my bills current I sometimes had to put off paying one of them altogether; so to make the repercussions as painless as possible, I would choose the one with the lowest late fee to rollover into next month's stack. I also may have postdated a few checks and hoped for the best.*

In such situations, we also have to **get extra resourceful with our resources** — by comparison shopping for cheaper brands, hunting for coupons, and/or waiting for deals. Or by using non-monetary resources — i.e., our time and energy — to pursue supplemental means of making ends meet. For my part, in order to augment my pitiful early-days publishing salary, I worked at a Broadway theater a couple of nights a week in the early 2000s. (This is how I met Cher, so I guess it wasn't all bad.) And even once my paycheck had become a bit more robust, I occasionally had to take on freelance editorial clients to make ends meet — especially when faced with similarly robust adult expenditures, like a wedding and honeymoon.

Again, I was fortunate to have those options, although TO BE

---

* For anyone under thirty reading this, "checks" are slips of paper that your parents used to send through the mail to pay their bills back in the olden days. Great system.

CLEAR, I also hate the fact that *any* of us have to consider holding down multiple jobs or killing ourselves with overtime just to get by or to have nice things — especially under circumstances far more brutal than taking tickets on a VIP rope line or marking up manuscripts till midnight on the weekend.

I said it before and I'll say it again: capitalism = scourge of the earth. **But at least with your TFG skills in full working order, you'll be better equipped to cope with it, and that's worth something.**

PRO-DULT TIP: No matter what else you serve at your budget dinner party, if you break a fancy chocolate bar into pieces and sprinkle it with sea salt for dessert, you become 50 percent more sophisticated.

Now let's imagine you've got a little more room in your budget. Like maybe enough to think about **SAVING?**

That'll add some **self-control** to the mix, plus a rendezvous with **our old chums, habits and incentives.** For example, by the time I was fifteen, I'd gotten a summer job — which meant that I could handle short-term budgeting for stuff like scrunchies and mall pizza, and also look toward longer-term, larger savings goals like taking part in a student exchange program to France, which I desperately wanted to do and for which I'd have to cough up the international airfare.

Helpfully, my dad had already laid down a strict **"one third, two thirds" policy** with regard to my waitressing paychecks. As in, one third in the bank, two thirds in my wallet — a mandated habit, but a **habit** nonetheless of regularly setting aside a portion of my income. And the prospect of munching baguettes in Bordeaux the next spring **provided a strong incentive** to build even further on those savings by adding the contents of my nightly tip jar to the France Fund.

If you can't swing a one-third reduction in your overall budget just to throw it in the bank, that's totally understandable. And if you don't *want* to commit to an amount that hefty, that's fine too. I won't tell my dad.

But if you *are* able and motivated to set aside *something*, then **getting into a habit can make the whole process** — wait for it — **EASIER and MORE PLEASANT!** It may take some effort to get started, but remember what we talked about in part I: with dedicated repetition, implementing a habit turns it from step 2 into "just a thing you do."

That adds up! And it may also take you back to **prioritizing**...

What if you want to put some money toward a goal — whether that's "making it rain" or just "saving for a rainy day" — but you don't have an easily identifiable extra chunk of change to allocate?

In that case, you'll have to take another look at your budget and decide if there's **something you're willing/able to sacrifice in service to your larger goal.**

And before anyone hoists their pitchforks, I'm well aware that we're all trying to exist within a system that's made it harder and harder for young people (or any people) to accumulate wealth, and I am IN NO WAY saying that broad financial freedom derives from forgoing an avo toast or a fancy latte three times a week. Only that, if your current budget includes $20 a month for a premium Netflix plan that you want but don't technically need, you *could* decide to cancel it in favor of saving toward something else you want *more*.

You're the adult here, so it's up to you.

When taxes attack!

Ye olde "one third, two thirds" savings plan also turned out to be a useful strategy when I went freelance in my forties and had to start dealing with my own tax withholding, aka the approximately 33 percent portion of your income the U.S. government is going to come for until you die or renounce your citizenship. (Maybe even then, who knows!) If you take no other advice from this chapter — nay, this entire book — take this, kids: DO NOT SLEEP ON YOUR WITHHOLDING. If your employer does not automatically set aside part of your paycheck for your friends at the IRS, then educate yourself about your tax bracket and squirrel that shit away for next April fifteenth. Quarterly estimates are tedious work, but I know people who've played fast and loose with the Tax Man, and let's just say that's a lesson in being held accountable for your actions that you do *not* want to have to learn the hard way.

Finally, with budgeting and saving well in hand, one day your good grownup work (and perhaps also your inherent privilege) may **unlock a whole other level of ADULT FINANCIAL FUN, such as** —

Retirement accounts!

Investments!

Mortgages!

Refinancing your mortgage at a lower rate — or maybe not bothering, since the world's probably gonna end before your thirty-year fixed is up anyway!

And each and every one of the above pursuits will **test your capacity for doing your homework and being resourceful** — e.g., studying up on interest rates and stock prices, or researching the kinds of people you could pay to do that shit for you. (Which'll add another line item to the budget, so keep that in mind.)

Additionally, navigating any complicated financial transaction will require you being able to **interact in a mature, polite and respectful manner** with bankers and lawyers and brokers and *all* of their assistants. (You do not want to piss off the people who are responsible for photocopying and submitting your documents on time.)

Oh, and that reminds me — keep your eyes peeled for **a little tip in part IV called "check your work."** There is no better time to do so than when you're filling out a co-op board package in hopes of scoring the apartment of your dreams in a competitive market. I have met co-op board presidents, and they DO NOT FUCK AROUND.

And that's about the size of it, my pretties. There are a million-and-two different scenarios and savings strategies and stock tips I or anyone could dole out — some of them sound as a pound and others as useless as a wooden nickel — but whether you're working with minimum wage or megabucks, it's those GTFU Greatest Hits burning a hole in your back pocket that'll serve you best, every time.

Good thing you've already spent a couple hundred pages boning up on those.

And now you're in the home stretch. How does it make you feel? Positively giddy with the anticipation of going out there and adulting your ass off, I hope! Or at least pretty cool? (I would accept "pretty cool.")

Anyway, you've done great work so far, and now it's **time to finish the last of your chores so you can go play.**

ACCOUNTABILITY, here we come.

IV

SORRY, MY BAD:

Owning up to what you did and stepping up to fix it

Here in part IV, all of your mature, responsible chickens are coming home to roost. You'll practice **living with the Cs of all those As and Bs, and holding yourself accountable** no matter what the outcome. Damn, you're good.

In the first half, on **OWNING UP,** you'll have a chance to prove how self-aware, honest, and polite you've become. Beginning with **"Come on, don't be like that,"** we'll deploy your most mature coping and communication skills to help you **take constructive criticism in stride.** Then, in **"Who let the dog out?,"** you'll practice **admitting fault** and **reducing your excuses** (bullshit and otherwise). And in **"Apologize to your sister!"** we'll go full-frontal adult by **learning how to say a sincere *I'm sorry.***

The second half is all about **STEPPING UP,** starting with one of Auntie Sarah's favorite chapters, **"Go clean your room."** Here we'll make use of earlier lessons in being self-sufficient and resourceful to aid you in **literally *and* figuratively mopping up your mess.** After that, you'll hop right back on the C-Cycle for some more fun with critical thinking. In **"Did you learn your lesson?"** I'll give you an uber-responsible strategy for **never making the mistake** in the first place; but if it happens anyway, I'll show you how to perform a **Reverse ABC** to figure out where you went wrong along the way…so you'll never make it *again*.

It's almost time to fire up that laminator, kids. You are *t-h-i-s* close to qualifying for your TFG card, **becoming an honest-to-goodness adult, AND getting treated like one.** I don't know about you, but I just got chills. Let's do this!

Owning up

Fun fact: nobody's perfect. Even those who write/or adhere to the teachings of an extraordinarily wise and practical book about adulting will still fuck up from time to time. That isn't such a problem; it's when we can't *own up* to our fuckups that we're in danger of regressing to the BFB Zone. And I say that with love, as someone who has had to work harder on accountability than all of the other adulting shit combined. Facing your flaws, owning your errors, and apologizing for your poor judgment or bad behavior? That's some high-level shit. But the good news is, if Auntie Sarah can learn to take criticism on the chin, admit when she's wrong, and say she's sorry, then so can you.

Come on, don't be like that

In part II, we talked about **maintaining self-control and communicating clearly and productively when somebody does ya dirty.** You mad, bro? Take a time-out, take a deep breath, strike a Power Pose, choose your words carefully, and deliver them coherently. That's how you hold *other people* accountable for *their* actions and behavior whilst remaining calm, poised, articulate, and respectful your own damn self.

Now it's time to **hold *yourself* accountable.** And that can be a little more difficult, so I thought I'd ease you in with everyone's favorite pastime: **taking constructive criticism without getting defensive.**

(Just kidding, we all know everyone's favorite pastime is watching that "Watermelon Sugar" video on repeat.)

Here's the thing: There will be many moments in life when someone is offering you genuine feedback, not an attack of the "you should def be mad, bro" variety. They're merely suggesting that you might could've done something differently and gotten a better outcome. Perhaps. *Maaaaaaybe.* **And said suggestion may not sit well, but that doesn't make it a war crime.**

The true test of your adulting mettle is how you **REACT** and **RESPOND.**

A BFB defaults to defense; whereas a TFG accepts that there could be something to this critique, and receives it in the same good faith in which it was intended. For example:

- **You make your opening statement in the debate tournament, and your coach mentions that you might come across as more authoritative if you didn't have to look down at your notes.**

A Big Fucking Baby gets defensive by way of denial: "They don't know what they're talking about. I never look down at my notes!"

A TFG says thanks, and takes *this* note under consideration.

- **You dream up a perfect South Beach bachelorette party for your BFF, and when you bring her the itinerary, she wonders aloud if it might be more fun to subtract the paddleboarding and add a stop at the club?**

A BFB plasters on their most passive-aggressive pout ("I mean, I put a lot of thought into this, but yeah, I guess if you want to do something *basic*…").

A TFG turns the page and says, "Sounds awesome, let me price out bottle service and get back to you!"

- **Your boss thinks the first draft of your proposal is great, but has a few suggestions for making your plan more cost-effective in the long run.**

A Big Fucking Baby gets their hackles up, gets indignant, and self-destructively refuses to make any changes.

A Total Fucking Grownup takes that feedback right back to the drawing board and gives it a whirl.

- **Your partner has an idea: maybe you could try a little something new to get their motor running?**

A Big Fucking Baby gets their feelings hurt ("Wow, this whole time I've been shitty in bed and you never said anything? I feel like such a loser") or worse, acts like a jerk ("I don't know, I think the problem here might be you").

A Total Fucking Grownup is willing to listen *and* take direction.

Theoretical Adults are somewhere in the middle, but veer closer to the BFB Zone a little more often than they'd probably care to admit. And I get it. **Even the most constructive, well-intentioned criticism can make you feel like you're not good enough, and *that* doesn't feel good at all.**

I can't really change how you feel, so what I'd like to do is help you *deal* with however you feel in the most adult manner possible — instead of, say, going scorched earth on a supervisor whose job is to supervise you, or throwing a counterproductive self-pity party when your partner suggests that your technique could use a touch of refinement.

To that end, here are **three tips for defusing your defense mechanisms** so you can first **REACT** and then **RESPOND** like a Total Fucking Grownup:

Listen to judgment without judgment

Before you decide whether you agree with the criticism — which, let's face it, the rules of "getting defensive" dictate that you almost certainly will not, at least not right away — the best first step is to take it all in without interrupting, crying, or theatrically removing your earrings. This is an excellent opportunity to revisit an early lesson in manner-minding, and just shut the fuck up and *listen*.

You're in this together

Both parties ultimately want the same thing here — be it a big win, an awesome night out, maximum profits, or mutually assured satisfaction. If you keep in mind that your performance (heh) and theirs are linked, you can take their critique less personally and approach it more productively. Remember: If you can dream it, you can team it! Or something like that.

Two things can be true AT THE SAME TIME

This a terrific all-around mantra that happens to be especially useful for taking criticism like a champ. For example: the temperature in the bedroom can be too cold for you AND too warm for your partner; you can be totally sick of this shit AND there can still be a worldwide pandemic raging; and you can be doing well AND still have room for improvement. Taking that last one into account will help you go from "Fuck that" to "Bring it on!" (while you secretly turn up the thermostat).

PRO-DULT TIP: On the topic of two things being true at once, you can *think* you know exactly where you're going and also be *very, very wrong.* Just. Fucking. Ask. For. Directions.

Once you've taken a beat to manage your **reaction,** you can proceed to take it all in and develop an appropriate grownup **response.** You've got a few options:

If you must admit there's merit in this critique of your actions and/or behavior, you say, "My, my, my, how right you are. Thanks!" and off you go to make some improvements. Look at you! So adult, so accountable.

If you're neutral on the suggestion in question, see above, replace "How right you are" with "Let me take another look at that," and see what shakes out. Giving due consideration to someone else's opinion can't hurt, and the mere appearance of doing so could *help* you quite a bit — especially when it involves "pleasing someone who signs your paychecks" or "not pissing off someone who shares your bed."

If, after nonjudgmental listening and thoughtful mulling, you still believe your way is the right way forward,

then that's your prerogative, but there's no need to go nuclear like a four-year-old who's been told her Wonder Woman Underoos are perhaps not appropriate attire for the family Christmas card shoot. An articulate, respectful response is the TFG's stock-in-trade.

- **For your coach:** "I hear what you're saying, but knowing how my brain works, I think I'd be worse off if I try to go completely off-book. I feel like I need to keep my notes handy."
- **For the bride:** You know what? Just do whatever she wants. It's her wedding.
- **For your boss:** "I really appreciate the feedback. I reran the numbers, and I actually think I've got the best profit margin there is. I'd like to present it this way, and I'll take full responsibility if the client disagrees."
- **For your sexy-time pal:** "I don't feel comfortable doing that. But maybe there's something else we'd *both* enjoy?"

Sticking with your gut can be a TFG move on its own — you've got self-awareness, critical thinking, decision-making, and all that good stuff going on — but remember: If you're going to talk the talk, you've gotta **commit to walking the walk and *remaining* accountable** no matter how things turn out. If the client balks or your partner walks, those consequences are yours to accept.

(And if it turns out that you were right all along, I'll caution you not to gloat your Big Fucking Baby butt off about it. Nobody likes *or* respects a poor sport.)

So that was our little amuse-bouche in accepting criticism even if you haven't done anything wrong, *per se*. Try it out, see how it feels. And then get ready for the main event: **admitting it when you *definitely* fucked up — and without making excuses for why.**

Who let the dog out?

In this chapter, we're assuming it was you. You let him out. And your only adult job here is to raise your hand, take your *tsk tsk,* and move on.

All of us are bound to make undeniable boo-boos from time to time — like when you overruled your teammates and lost the pub trivia championship because you were SO SURE that *Get Out* won the Oscar for Best Picture in 2017.* It's not "constructive criticism" when the trivia emcee reads "*The Shape of Water*" off the card. It's

---

* Probably because it *should* have.

just the facts. And it should be easy enough (if a little embarrassing) to cop to your brain fart, take a modicum of good-natured ribbing from your friends, and move on.

So why is it, then, that a recurring beef among my survey responders was with **"people who always make excuses instead of just admitting to their mistakes"**? This came up a lot, which suggests that far too many of us are inclined to go down swinging with weak explanations — or worse, bullshit lies — to cover our asses when we blow it bigtime.

Once again, I do understand the impulse. I believe I confessed on page 31 of this very book that I have a hard time admitting fault. I suspect this is because for basically my entire childhood I pinned my sense of self-worth on being a Little Miss Know-It-All/teacher's pet — such that **to be wrong about *anything* felt like an existential failure.**

Good times.

Anyway, let's get the "bullshit lies" out of the way first. This is an easy fix. **If you fucked up, it was most definitely all your fault, and everybody knows it,** then your best chance at redemption is to 'fess up like a TFG instead of trying to weasel out of it like a BFB. To wit:

LIAR, LIAR

THING YOU FUCKED UP	DON'T SAY	DO SAY
Remembering your mom's birthday	"I called twice but I didn't catch you."	"Oh shit, I totally forgot."
Snuck out of work early and got caught	"I asked Bob if I could take off."	"Busted."
Failing to turn in your paper for Philosophy 101	"My dog ate my homework."	"I'll have it for you tomorrow, Professor."

Pfft. Your mom may be old, but she knows how to check her call logs; Bob wasn't on duty that night; and your dog doesn't even like Socrates. Stop LYING, Liar.

Now let's get into mildly more gray territory, such as when something goes wrong on your watch and you know better than to lie about it, but you still **can't quite bring yourself to admit it was your fault and fully OWN UP to your role.**

Master Equivocators dance *around* the truth to avoid self-incrimination. Again, an easy fix:

MASTER EQUIVOCATOR

THING YOU FUCKED UP	DON'T SAY	DO SAY
Paying your rent on time	"No! It can't possibly be the 15th already, can it?"	"I'm doing the transfer now."
Showing up for the meeting	"Weird. I'm not sure I was on that email?"	"Oops, I never put it in my calendar."
Doing 85 mph in a 55-mph zone	"Maybe your radar gun is on the fritz?"	"Here's my license and registration, Officer. It won't happen again."

And finally, we've got the **Excuse Makers.** They don't lie, or even avoid the truth of the fuckup itself, but they always seem to have a reason why things didn't work out that [they think] *excuses* their actions and behavior.

Is this the worst quality a person could have? No. But it is deeply aggravating to others, and paints you as less than the Total

FG I know you can be. **And if you can admit to exhibiting this bad habit, then you can commit to breaking it.**

How?

When you're tempted to offer an extenuating explanation for the reason why you whiffed, ask yourself:

Is this a reasonable *reason?*

Because plenty of excuses that aren't out-and-out lies still do not *excuse* you from culpability. Total Fucking Grownups know that **explanation is not justification, and that furthermore, nobody wants to hear it.**

For example: Is it *technically* true that an unexpected overtime rally by your favorite basketball team caused you to get home an hour later last night than you'd anticipated, and that is, in fact, what prevented you from being able to finish the client presentation that was due this morning? Sure, okay.

But if pressed, would you also have to admit you shouldn't have pushed this deadline so far that one hour was going to make or break your ability to meet it? Yuppers.

When your reason is not so reasonable, owning up and then *shutting up* — no excuses — is your best course of action. It's not as though people are going to look much more kindly on a Theoretical Adult who lets the Washington Wizards' fourth-quarter

> ### Unreasonable reasons for why you fucked up
>
> Accidentally got way too high
> Don't believe in alarm clocks
> Mercury is in retrograde
> Stopped to pet a cat

comeback dictate their productivity level than they would a BFB who skipped straight to "I just didn't feel like it."

A *reasonable* reason is far more rare. And it still probably won't "excuse" your behavior, but it may explain it in a way that makes you look like slightly less of an asshole or makes someone else feel slightly better about the whole thing. You're going to have to use your judgment on that. (Better judgment than you used to get yourself *into* this situation, that is.)

For example, if you just went full Karen on the barista at Dunkin' and the "reason" for your ugly outburst was "I clearly asked for *ALMOND* MILK," that's a no-no.

But if you lost your cool and got snippy because your mom is in the hospital and you're really worried about her and haven't slept in thirty-six hours and you're at the end of your rope, well, that's more reasonable, and if you want to go back inside and offer up that explanation-not-justification as part of your penance, it's your call.

(Either way, you should say you're sorry. You were way out of line, whatever the reason.)

Apologize to your sister!

I should start by saying that if apologizing is something you're already good at, I salute you, because it's not always easy to eat crow. Plucking the feathers alone is *such* a hassle. Still, if one wants to be a Total Fucking Grownup, one must find a way to show up and take accountability for one's actions and behavior. Full stop. It's not 33.3 percent of the GTFU MO for nothin'.

And believe me, I know from extensive personal experience that prostrating yourself before Those You've Wronged, Disappointed, or Pissed Off can be **anxiety-inducing** and **embarrassing**, and it can **make you feel small.** Even though being an adult means accepting that sometimes you just *hafta* do things that may not feel so good, this one is a real kick in the teeth, even if it's absolutely the right way forward.

Hm. I wonder if there's some way to make doing the right thing, say, a little easier? Perhaps a bit more pleasant? Or, I dunno, if there could be some relief in it for you?

In fact, I think I might be onto something here...

What if you woke up tomorrow and decided that apologizing felt *GOOD?*

- **What if, instead of feeling anxious, you felt LIBERATED?** Apologizing is a great way to put an end to the feedback loop and free yourself from the negative self-talk that's likely to keep you up at night for much longer than it takes to say, "I'm sorry. Can you forgive me?"

- **What if, instead of feeling embarrassed, you felt EMPOWERED?** Sure, you fucked up, but what's done is done. This is your chance to take back control of the narrative and start fresh.

- **What if, instead of feeling small for having fucked up, you felt like a BIG WINNER for being the kind of person who can acknowledge and apologize for it?** Frankly, any day you can do *that* is a day that you, my friend, are the adultiest adult in the room. Humble yourself and be proud.

If you can **shift your mind-set** to think of apologizing as a feel-good activity *in addition* to a do-good activity, it becomes that much EASIER and MORE PLEASANT to engage in whenever the need arises. (At least, that's what works for me — plus the fact that my husband is infuriatingly good at this shit and I've always been motivated by a bit of healthy competition.) And then unlike the kindergartners and surly teens, some Theoretical Adults, and *all* the BFBs who walk among us, you'll never again need to be coached, prodded, or guilt-tripped into apologizing to your sister for having cut the sleeves off her favorite dress and used them as bedding for your pet rabbit because "Lord Flopsy likes the feel of velvet on his tummy."

A true TFG knows what they did, why they shouldn't have done it, and what they need to say to start making things right.

Fortunately, once you've summoned the adult wherewithal to speak them, coming up with the words themselves isn't nearly as hard. Auntie Sarah's got you covered:

WAY TO APOLOGIZE	POTENTIAL ADD-ON
I'm sorry.	I will fix this.
I'm sorry.	I promise it won't happen again.
I'm sorry.	What can I do to make it up to you?
I'm sorry.	I should have listened.
I'm sorry.	You were right, I was wrong.
I'm sorry.	And for what it's worth, Lord Flopsy is too.

Once you get in the groveling groove, you can try upping the ante from delivering **after-the-fact acts of contrition** to honing your **in-the-moment ability to de-escalate.** Like so:

When your neighbor calls to complain about your loud music, a sincere "So sorry about that! We'll turn it down!" can take the wind out of their angry sails *before* they move on to calling the cops.

A preemptive and heartfelt midargument "I know, I know, I messed up" can soften your partner's hardest heart *before* they kick you out. (Or at least before they change the locks.)

A hastily scrawled note of remorse passed across the table to your boss after you royally bungle that conference call can short their fuse *before* it has a chance to completely blow.

I'm telling you, kids: go into Mea Culpa Mode — the sooner the better — and you'll be unstoppable!

PRO-DULT TIP: Contrary to what multi–Grammy Award–winning artist and cocreator of virtual DJ battle web series *Verzuz* Timbaland would have you believe, it's never too late to apologize. In fact, finally busting out a long overdue "My bad" can completely transform, repair, and resurrect relationships and reputations. And it feels good too.

In sum: apologizing — when it's warranted — is adult AF.

It is mature to the max.

It is responsible in the extreme.

And above and beyond all those good feelz and better outcomes I've laid out, a swift, sincere "I'm sorry" is likely to garner you the **understanding** and maybe even **forgiveness** of Those You've Wronged, Disappointed, or Pissed Off — all of which leads to the biggest reward of all for anyone who has ever royally fucked up:

A second chance.

Sorry, NotSorry

As important as knowing when and how to apologize is for maintaining your integrity and relationships, it's equally important — for your own sanity and sense of self-worth — to know when you do *not* owe anyone an apology. That is, when you haven't done anything wrong and needn't be guilted by yourself or anyone else into thinking you did! My Not-Sorry Method (from *The Life-Changing Magic of Not Giving a Fuck* and featured prominently in my TEDx Talk) allows that as long as you conduct yourself honestly and politely in service of sticking to your boundaries and meeting your own needs, then you have nothing to apologize FOR. Remember that the next time someone gets on your case for not doing something that you already quite clearly and politely told them you had NO INTENTION OF DOING. Sheesh.

And now I've got a little secret: As far as I'm concerned, you, my fine feathered fuckling, just made it through the toughest leg of the adulting gauntlet. Seriously, if the first half of part IV was the Olympic decathlon, the back end is like a leisurely round of mini-golf on a sunny day.

Owning up can be thorny and emotionally taxing. Stepping up is just details. And once you sort out those details, you can get to work collecting on all the incentives you promised yourself as a reward for finishing this book.

Deal?

Stepping up

This is where we close the loop on holding yourself accountable for your actions and behavior, and facing the consequences in full. Because making amends won't always end with "I was wrong" or even "I'm sorry." Sometimes you'll have to repair the damage in a more tangible way — such as fixing something you broke, replacing something you lost, or enacting a series of more responsible actions and mature behavior to regain someone's trust over time. And no matter what, if any, cleanup your fuckup hath wrought, the stepping up doesn't end until you've learned your lesson, so you don't have to do it all over again. (And again.)

Go clean your room

Full disclosure: Auntie Sarah is a very tidy bitch, and will absolutely judge you for storing your clean shirts on the floor or your
dirty dishes in the sink. That said, I have also gone on record in
several venues asserting that whatever matters most to you — or in
this case, doesn't matter at all — should take precedence over anyone else's *opinion* about how you choose to live your life.

If you don't mind living in filth (or even mild disarray), and it's
not hurting anybody else, fine. You do you.* Much as I would like
to find a way to justify it, I cannot claim that being an adult is predi-
cated on being a neat freak.

But when it comes to growing the fuck up, we still need to
talk about **other kinds of messes you might make — ones that
do affect other people — and how taking accountability FOR
them includes cleaning up AFTER them.**

An Actual Baby lets other people pick up their pieces because
they themselves *cannot*.

---

* While I break into a cold sweat thinking about that half bottle of Gatorade
you're "storing" under your bed.

A Big Fucking Baby assumes other people will do their dirty work, because they themselves suck.

A Theoretical Adult lacking in the proactive, self-sufficient department *waits and hopes* for someone else to take care of their mess, because that would be easier. Not cool, buddy, not cool.

A Total Fucking Grownup takes charge, takes initiative, and gets resourceful with this shit.

For example:

- **Imagine you show up at work this morning and discover that your company's website is down...and it's your fault. Whoopsie!**

I know it's nerve-wracking, but TFGs (especially ones who've gotten this far in this book) have the tools to mitigate their emotions and get to work on those details I mentioned. Perhaps it's time to make a lovely, calming list? Or simply time to get on the phone or into the chat window with your site provider to find out what steps you can take to make things right — and then take them! If that means shifting some other less urgent work off your schedule, then roll over, Beethoven, because you just added "reprioritizing" to the list of adult actions you've taken today. Nice one.

- **You borrowed a friend's car and got in a wreck. You're okay, but the Fiat is fucked.**

This is a sucky situation for all concerned, but whether or not you were at fault for the accident itself, you're on the hook for dealing with the fallout. Explanation is not justification, and all that.

If you had permission to borrow the car (PLEASE TELL ME YOU HAD PERMISSION), and your friend has insurance (PLEASE TELL ME THEY HAVE INSURANCE), then it's probably covered — but still, somebody has to do all the paperwork and wait on hold with the insurance company as long as it takes to get the claim processed, and that someone is you.

Oh, and your friend is going to need transport for the next couple of weeks while their car is in the shop, so anything you can do to secure them a loaner, or chauffeur them around? Do it.

- **Even though you love them, you've been foolishly ignoring your partner's expressed needs for so long that the relationship is officially on life support.**

PRO-DULT TIP: Renters insurance is so cheap — and so worth it — for the protection and peace of mind you get in return. Some landlords will require that you carry it, but even if they don't, you should check it out. In addition to being able to easily replace stuff that gets damaged or stolen (and you *know* you can't live without your phone or laptop for very long), you can be reimbursed for living expenses if you have to move out due to water damage, for example; or for medical and legal expenses for you (or someone else) who gets injured in your home; and you can "schedule" extras like expensive jewelry to be covered as needed. (Hello, engagement rings!)

This problem is not going to fix itself, and it most certainly isn't on the other party to fix *for* you. Furthermore, it's probably going to take more than a one-time gesture (even a grand one) to reverse the trend and repair the damage.

If you got to this point because you're not so good at picking up on clues or following through on promises, then I suggest you reread part II, for starters. It sounds like you could use a refresher course on self-awareness, active listening, and being considerate, plus maybe a new habit of spending Sunday mornings talking to your beloved over coffee instead of staring at your phone? And then perhaps you could brush up on "doing what you said you would do, when you said you would do it." I've heard that works wonders.

> ### 6 tips for keeping your actual room clean, because I cannot help myself
>
> 1. Count your shirts. X = total number of shirts you own. Obtain X-plus-ten hangers. There, no more clean shirts on the floor. It's like *magic*.
> 2. For the dirty ones, it's called a hamper. H-a-m-p-e-r. Look into it.
> 3. A decent vacuum cleaner is a friend for life. (And a cordless hand-held will do in a pinch. I love my Shark WANDVAC more than most people love their children.)
> 4. If more of us had been using those 20-percent-off coupons to buy Swiffer dusters from Bed Bath & Beyond, maybe it wouldn't be going out of business.
> 5. Like Chekhov's gun, if a coaster appears on the table in Act I, it better get used.
> 6. I honestly can't believe I have to say this, but unless you love getting crumbs in your butt crack: STOP EATING IN BED. Just stop it.

Of course, one hopes that if you've been paying attention and soaking up all the good stuff *Grow the Fuck Up* has to offer, then future messes — literal *and* figurative — will be kept to a happy minimum. **But if and when the time comes to 'fess up AND step up, the most effective way to play is very simple, and it is as follows:**

1. Do it ASAP

The longer you leave a stain to set, the harder it is to get it out, and the same is true for more metaphorical spills and splotches. If you know what you did wrong, other people probably do too. And every day you make your sister wait before you return the Jimmy Choos you did *not* have permission to borrow is another day that she'll have in which to plot her revenge.

2. Do it well

You're about to spend more time, energy, and/or money to fix something you *already* spent time, energy, and/or money breaking. Don't set yourself up for round three by doing a half-assed job of it. Auntie Sarah taught you better than that.

3. And do it yourself

For the same reason you should *immediately* and *aggressively* attend to that toilet you clogged at the yoga retreat: BECAUSE OTHER PEOPLE SHOULDN'T HAVE TO.

Next up, last licks on taking your licks like a Total Fucking Grownup.

Did you learn your lesson?

I'm going to close the book on being an accountable adult by showing you a super-easy way to retrace your steps and figure out where you went wrong, so it never happens again. It's real good stuff. But first, how **about a neat trick for avoiding making a mistake in the first place?**

Check your work

Growing up, this was one of my dad's go-to refrains. Which tracks, since he was an elementary school teacher who had to grade twenty-five book reports and math tests at a clip and was therefore eminently familiar with **the kinds of errors that a thorough proofread or quick recalculation could have prevented.**

I confess that when directed at ME (a straight-A student who ate extra credit for breakfast), I considered those three little words a micromanaging of my already heroic homework endeavors — but still, the man was onto something. "Check your work" has served me well for decades, and it's not just for spelling tests and geometry proofs anymore.

There are many situations in your adult life where **a**

simple once-over will save you a whole lotta heartbreak. Five minutes of carefully double-checking an invoice or an itinerary is a lot less hassle than dealing with the fallout after you ship a package to the wrong address or summon your ride to the wrong airport.

PRO-DULT TIP: If you have a smartphone with a "world clock" feature, you need never be bamboozled by time zones again. I can't tell you how many years I spent trying to do quick mental math when making travel reservations or scheduling a call with a foreign counterpart before I realized my iPhone would just *tell me* what the fuck time it was in London. Amazing.

Does going back to ensure you dotted all your i's and crossed all your t's before you hit PURCHASE add what you may consider an annoying step to the process? Perhaps, but ordering the wrong size sofa and booking nonrefundable plane tickets for the wrong day are even less fun, son.

Think of checking your work as holding yourself accountable TO yourself, before a potential fuckup even has a chance to occur.

And we're not aiming for "perfectionism-induced paranoia paralysis" here — just, like, making sure you scheduled your boss's press conference for the ballroom at the Four Seasons Hotel, not the parking lot of Four Seasons Total Landscaping; or that the sexy text you're about to send contains the correct recipient in the To: field. (One way to avoid *that* stomach-churning moment is to simply remove the professional acquaintance named "Jud" from your contacts for the sole purpose of never almost-accidentally sending him private correspondence meant for your husband, "Judd." Not that I would know anything about it.)

Yes, my T F'ing Gs, Mr. Knight had it right from jump street. Checking your work and **looking twice before you leap will save you time, energy, money, aggravation, and embarrassment** — and it'll save other people all of that too, be they taxi drivers, big bosses, or just unsuspecting literary agents named Jud.

And now, as promised, the final step toward stepping up...

<drumroll>

I present to you: the **Reverse ABC!**

It's as easy as C, B, A

One reason this step is so easy is because I already showed you how to do it way back on page 38. Now all you have to do is reverse it, **and *that's* how you learn your lesson.**

To perform a **Reverse ABC, start with the real-life**

CONSEQUENCES of whatever mistake you made, and then **work backward to pinpoint the BEHAVIOR and ACTIONS that got you there.** Remember what I said earlier about critical thinking and collecting data from your lived experience: the benefit of hindsight is increased foresight. **Today's CBAs become tomorrow's ABCs, and your outcomes are looking rosier than ever.** For example:

> **CONSEQUENCES:** The work website going down was not only horrifying, it was a *bitch* to fix.

> **BEHAVIOR and/or ACTIONS THAT GOT YOU HERE:** Turns out, you missed an email last week from your provider letting you know that they would be changing servers and you'd need to fiddle with the DNS or something (I don't know, I'm just spitballing here) to make sure the site *you* were responsible for got ported properly.

> Now, why'd you miss the email? Did it go to your junk folder? If so…

> **WHAT HAVE YOU LEARNED?** You should mark that sender "safe" to avoid a repeat performance, and then scroll

through the rest of your spam and do the same for any other important missives that may have gotten stuck there. Also, maybe you should make it a HABIT to peep that folder once a week or so, just in case? There, that was easy.

(Whereas if you missed the memo when it was right there in your inbox — because you're not keeping a very close eye on things — then "what you've learned" is that you ought to stop playing fast and loose with important correspondence instead of just "hoping it won't happen again," which is the MO of BFBs the world over.)

Here are a couple more examples to get your Reverse ABCs up to speed:

CONSEQUENCES: You ran out of gas on the roadside and had to walk six miles round trip to a gas station for a can of regular unleaded.

BEHAVIOR and/or ACTIONS THAT GOT YOU HERE: It wasn't even because you couldn't afford to fill up in this wretched economy; you just ignored the indicator longer than you knew you should have. Goddammit.

WHAT HAVE YOU LEARNED? That little red light is there for a reason, it is not to be trifled with, and procrastination will give you blisters.

CONSEQUENCES: You wasted your third bag of unused baby spinach this month, *and* you had to clean stinky rotten spinach goo out of the fridge drawer. Yuck.

BEHAVIOR and/or ACTIONS THAT GOT YOU HERE: Once again, you bought fresh produce without a plan for cooking it before it went bad.

WHAT HAVE YOU LEARNED? I'm guessing the answer is "Menu plan first, *then* grocery store" or "I cannot be trusted to eat fresh produce and should just stop pretending I care about salad." Maybe both!

I've been saying it all along. Your actions and behavior have consequences, and YOU have the power to influence those consequences by thinking everything through ahead of time — but if you didn't quite manage to do that, **the Reverse ABC is your second chance to make a Totally Fucking Grownup impression.**

What did I tell you? Easy as taking candy from an Actual Baby.

* * *

And there you have it, kiddo. You are officially primed to go out and adult your ass off. I'm so proud of you for making it this far! And I must admit, I'm excited to watch as the years go by and this sweary little book inspires an army of my favorite fucklings to rise to the mature, responsible, accountable occasion — and maybe even save the world while they're at it. As you know, Auntie Sarah is hoping to retire under halfway decent global circumstances, so thanks in advance for anything you can do to help make that happen. You're the best!

PRO-DULT TIP: With regard to our earlier talk of "knowing how to use Saran Wrap without wanting to throw it across the room in a fit of rage," I've conducted some empirical research on this topic and here is the conclusion I've reached: Saran Wrap is the devil's work. Cast it out of your life and don't look back. There are other ways to keep food fresh and keep onion smell out of your fridge. Those restaurant-style half-pint/pint/quart containers with interchangeable lids? Life-changing! Same advice goes for "knowing how to fold fitted sheets," BTW. Just roll 'em up and stuff 'em in the drawer. I'll never tell.

EPILOGUE: Everybody try!

Remember when you would go on long car trips as a kid, and your parents would encourage you to "just try" to use the bathroom before leaving home?

That's because they had the presence of mind to think ahead, anticipate consequences, and take responsible action to orchestrate the best outcome for all involved — which was a) not having to make an unscheduled, out-of-the-way stop at a sketchy gas station and b) not having any accidents on the upholstery.

Sometimes their ploy worked, you were able to go, and off you went. Other times your bladder simply would not cooperate until you were cruising down the interstate without an off-ramp in sight, and you'd have to beg your father to pull over before you wet both yourself and the front seat of his Nissan, and he would tell you that it can't possibly be that bad and this is why we try before we get in the car (which you did!!!) and now you're just going to have to hold it.

Thirty years later you will remain royally peeved about that interaction and take the opportunity to put him on blast for it in your book, but because you are a MATURE ADULT, you will also fashion this anecdote into a teachable moment for your readers.

As such, I'd like to leave you with one last observation about what it takes to be all grown up.

Life, you see, is basically one long road trip. And now that you're the adult in the driver's seat, it's up to you to navigate on your own behalf, of your own free will, and under your own power. You plan the route. You pack the car. You fill the tank. And you get yourself from point A to point Z on schedule — or as close to on time as possible, having almost certainly encountered and surmounted some unexpected detours along the way.

Or at least you *try*.

That's it. That's the secret to being an adult and getting treated like one. I even gave you a little hint in the flowchart on page 71, where every effort to "try again" leads you down a path toward that TFG life. Of course, I hope you'll go out there and take a whole bunch of the extremely useful, specialized advice I've offered in these pages, but honestly? If you can just prove that you're willing to *try*, then no one shall ever again have cause to curse your name in an anonymous survey about Big Fucking Babies and their bad fucking attitudes.

Total Fucking Grownups figure out what they want and at least try to go get it.

Total Fucking Grownups see a need and at least try to meet it.

Total Fucking Grownups have problems and at least try to find solutions.

Total Fucking Grownups get disappointed and at least try to get over it.

Total Fucking Grownups make mistakes and at least try to learn from them.

Sometimes the literal or metaphorical wheels will come off. Sometimes you'll take a wrong turn or run out of gas. And sometimes, despite your diligent attempt, nothing came out on the front end, and now you're going to have to stop at the highway McDonald's to use their McRestroom.

C'est la pee, as the French say. These things happen. Even the T-est of F-ing Gs don't succeed at *everything, all the time.* But as long as you commit to remaining self-aware and practicing self-control, thinking things through as best you can and taking initiative when you can, and being reliable, resourceful, and willing to own up to and clean up after your messes when you make 'em...therein lies all the evidence Auntie Sarah needs that you have grown the fuck up.

Good job. At least you tried.

JUST LIKE I DID BEFORE WE GOT IN THE CAR, DAD.

GROW

THE

FUCK

UP!

Acknowledgments

I'm not sure it takes a village to publish a book so much as it takes a team of wildly intelligent, creative, enterprising gluttons for punishment — but either way, between my teams at CAA (formerly ICM Partners) and Hachette Book Group, I've got the best/longest-suffering squad on my side. *Grow the Fuck Up* is our tenth (!) book together, and to all of them — along with the booksellers and readers who've kept the NFG machine rolling along all these years — I say: Oops!...We did it again.

(And THANK YOU.)

My agent, Jennifer Joel, is by far the adultiest adult in every room, and I'm extraordinarily lucky to have her as a friend, an advocate, and an "in" at many fine restaurants in New York City. She is truly a triple threat.

My editor, Michael Szczerban at Voracious, is smart, funny, and kind, which are my three favorite qualities in any human, let alone one whose job it is to tell me everything I'm doing wrong and help me make it better. His big, beautiful brain has left its mark on every page of every NFGG.

At Quercus Books, we gained a new partner in crime, Zöe Blanc, who helped bring *Grow the Fuck Up* to fruition in the UK and Ireland while my longtime editor Jane Sturrock had her hands full ushering a new future reader into the fold. Thank you for all of your efforts, Zöe, and I'm sorry I had to be the one to introduce you to the concept of "ass on a cracker."

As for the rest of the Total Fucking Grownups who spent their days making GTFU happen (and in most cases, many more NFGGs besides), all my appreciation goes to these fine folks:

Sindhu Vegesena, Lindsay Samakow, Loni Drucker, and Josie Freedman at CAA.

Thea Diklich-Newell, Juliana Horbachevsky, Jessica Chun, Ben Allen, Barbara Perris, Craig Young, Brandon Kelley, Laura Mamelok, Zoe Morgan-Weinman, Bruce Nichols, Kini Allen, Melissa Mathlin, and Stacey Schuck of Voracious/Little, Brown; Lisa Cahn and Michelle Figueroa of Hachette Audio; and special thanks to newly freelance designer Lauren Harms for lending her considerable talents (and handwriting) to each and every NFGG, including the magnificent full backlist refresh that's coming soon to bookstores near you.

Ana McLaughlin, Lisa Gooding, Lipfon Tang, Dave Murphy, Katy Follain, and Jon Butler of Quercus; as well as the dear departed (from Quercus, not from this realm) Charlotte Fry, who never met an email of mine she couldn't answer in ten seconds flat. I miss you, Charlotte! And many thanks to Luke Bird, Andrew Smith, and Tash Webber for creating and producing the super cool UK cover that all the kids will be talking about in 2023.

I'm also incredibly lucky to have had the ongoing support of Hachette teams in Canada, Ireland, Australia, and New Zealand, along with more than thirty publishers worldwide who've been spreading the word in translation, book by book, since 2015. Thank you all so much, and please know that I do not take one single copy in one single language in one single country for granted. Nor, for that matter, one single reader.

Big ups to *my* cool aunties, who taught me well: Rayette, Felicia, Nella, and Donna.

Penultimate but not least: thank you to my parents, Tom and Sandi Knight, whose collective wisdom permeates these pages; and to my brother, Tom, and my sister-in-law, Becky, for providing the ultimate inspiration for a book about growing the fuck up in the form of my nephew, Robert. Long may he reign.

And finally, as always, thank you to my personal, perpetual supply of reward and relief: the one and only Judd Harris.

Index

Page numbers in *italics* indicate illustrations.

accountability, 16, 70
  admitting when you fucked up,
    237–42
  apologizing and, 242–48
  as part of GTFU MO, 17, 18, 40
  stepping up and, 249–50
  to yourself, 230, 236–37, 257
Actual Babies, 27, 45, 51, 104, 124,
    158, 250
  communication and, 46
  consequences and, 38
  emotions of, 79
  in evolution of Total Fucking
    Grownups, 26
  immaturity of, 27
advance planning, 193–95, 199–201,
    204–7
"Am I acting like a fucking adult?"
    flowchart, 71, 264
apologizing, 242–48
  mind-set about, 243–45
  NotSorry Method and, 247

aprons, 36
articulateness, 127–29, 230
audience, know your, 135–36

baby showers, 162, 163
bad cop, being your own, 88–89
Beyoncé, 129, 200
Big Fucking Babies (BFBs),
    27–28, 45, 104, 211–12,
    251, 260
  anonymous survey on, 28, 30–31,
    265
  apologizing and, 244
  in evolution of Total Fucking
    Grownups, 26
  failure to own up, 229, 242
  gloating by, 237
  initiative of, 162
  job interviews and, 46–47,
    49, 52
  mistakes of, 238
  reaction to criticism, 231, 232

Big Fucking Babies (BFBs) *(cont.)*
   taking advantage of help from
      others, 158
   whining and, 131, 135
birthdays, forgetting, 239
biting your tongue, 105–7
bosses
   apologizing to, 246
   brainstorming ways to improve
      circumstances with,
      133–34
   honesty with, 87, 89
   politeness towards, 106–7
   reaction to criticism from, 232,
      233, 236
   respecting boundaries of, 140–41
   taking initiative with, 165
   whining about, 132, 135
boundaries, respecting, 76, 136–41
breast self-exams, 57
breathing, deep, 124–25
brides, 236
budgets, 169, 216–18, 222

calm, techniques for remaining,
   116–23
Calm the Fuck Down (Knight), 10,
   122, 148
C-Cycle, 45–54, *54*
   communication in, 48–50, 54
   confidence and, 69
   coping in, 51–53, 54, 113–16
   critical thinking in, 46–48, 53–54
checking your work, 223, 256–58
Cher, 218

cleaning up after yourself, 35–36,
   250, 254
co-op board packages, 223
colleagues
   politeness towards, 101
   respecting, 103
communication
   articulateness and, 127–29
   in C-Cycle, 48–50, 54
   in job interviews, 49–50
   with romantic partners, 87, 90–91,
     128, 132–33
   while checking your privilege,
     92–97
compliments, 107–8, 112
confidence, 68–69
conflict, being diplomatic during,
   109
consequences, 38–40
   anticipating, 153–57
   bad, avoiding, 41–42, 43
   conquering, 41–44
   coping with, 51–53, 54
   critical thinking about, 46, 53–54
   in Reverse ABC, 258–61
consideration, 110–12
constructive criticism, 230–37
Consumer Reports, 213
coping, 51–53, 54
   articulateness and, 127–29
   in job interviews, 52–53
   poise and, 124–27
   self-control and, 113–16
   self-soothing techniques, 116–23
   and showing respect, 129–31

Corden, James, 28
coworkers
    respecting boundaries of, 138
    whining to, 132
critical thinking, 12, 53–54, 140, 159,
            177, 259
    in dealing with money, 216, 217
    in job interviews, 46–48
criticism, constructive, 230–37
CrossFit, 182
Cuddy, Amy, 125

deadlines, work, 112
decisions
    independence and acting on,
            152–57
    value-based, 148–52
Decoding Spanish Wine, 61
deep breathing, 124–25
delegating, 158–59
dependability, 192–210
    advance planning and, 193–95,
            199–201, 204–7
    being on time, 204–7
    doing your homework, 211–14, 222
    money and, 214–23
        critical thinking in, 216, 217
        prioritizing, 216, 217–18, 220
        resourcefulness in, 216, 222
        saving, 219–21
    prioritizing and, 207–10
    tips for, 195–203
        don't overcommit, 195–96,
            206–7
        listmaking, 202–3

looking at week in advance, 201
managing expectations, 197–98
running through plans the night
        before, 200–201
setting expectations, 196–97
dessert, 219
dinner parties, 219
diplomacy, 109–10, 113
directions, asking for, 235
disappointment, expressing, 113–14
doctors, 183–85
dressing for success, 126–27
due diligence, 35, 47
dusting, 57

eating, 81, 82, 85, 86, 254
eating disorders, 182
education
    debt and, 151
    decisions about, 156
email addresses, 51
emotional clarity, 79–86
entry-level positions, 103
Excuse Makers, 240–42
excuses, 238
expectations
    managing, 197–98
    setting, 196–97

family, asking for forgiveness from, 90
Farrow, Ronan, 172
financial management
    dependability and, 214–23
    self-sufficiency and, 160
    See also money

financial remuneration, 130
first aid supplies, 183
fitted sheets, 262
food allergies, 182
freelancing and taxes, 221
friends
    honesty with, 87–88
    politeness towards, 105
    respecting boundaries of, 139
    stepping up after causing
        inconvenience for, 252
Fuck No! (Knight), 10, 110, 141

gender
    honorifics relating to, 99
    as limiting access, 93, 94, 95
Get Your Shit Together (Knight), 10,
    146, 148, 207
Goo Gone, 21, 29
grocery shopping, 158, 159, 160
GTFU MO (growing the fuck up
    modus operandi), 16–18,
    38–39, 40
GTFU MO-tivation, 33–37, 99
    habits and, 61
    politeness and, 99

habits, 56–64, 67, 180, 219,
    220, 260
hangers, 81, 82, 85
health
    mental, 186–91
    physical, 174–81
        alcohol habits and, 178–79
        first aid supplies and, 183

    getting and going to a doctor,
        183–85
    ignoring other people's notions
        about, 181–82
    no one-size fits-all prescription
        for, 175–76
    sexual health, 177–78
    sleep and, 177
Hodgkin, Dorothy, 172
homework
    doing, 211–14, 222
    failure to turn in, admitting, 239
honesty
    about wants and needs with others,
        87–91
    about your role in a problem, 135
    with audience, 87–88
    as the best policy, 78–79
    in communication, 89–91
    as pillar of No Fucks Given ethos,
        75, 99
    self-awareness and, 79, 80–84, 87,
        89–91
    with yourself, 79, 87
houseguests, 101–2
how/why/what method, 80–86

IKEA furniture, 170
in-laws, future, 101
incentives, 56, 65–67, 219, 220
independence, 147
    decisions and, 152–57
    and making shit happen, 157–60,
        166
    prioritizing and, 148–49, 150–51

resourcefulness and, 166–73
and taking initiative, 160–65
value-based decisions and,
148–52
initiative, taking
independence and, 160–65
mental health and, 188–89
insurance, renters, 253
integrity, 15, 75, 91, 247
invitations, RSVP to, 110

job interviews
communication and, 49–50
coping after, 52–53
critical thinking and,
46–48
email addresses used for, 51
jobs, multiple, 218–19

kindness, 16, 112
Knight, Robert Ray, 12, 70
Knight, Sarah
accountability and, 229
as "the anti-guru," 10, 11–13
apologizing and, 244
asserting self at work, 7, 60–61
attitude about eating, 182
augmenting of early-days
publishing salary, 218, 219
broken hand of, while on a
deadline, 170
Calm the Fuck Down, 10, 122, 148
car trips as a child, 263–64, 266
current lifestyle of, 10
difficulty admitting fault, 31, 238

father of, 213, 256, 263–64
freelancing and, 218, 219, 221
Fuck No!, 10, 110, 141
Get Your Shit Together, 10, 146,
148, 207
as a Goody-Two Shoes, 137
habits of, 57–58, 59–60
health care and, 183–84, 185
healthy living and, 175–76
leaving career as a book editor, 10
*The Life-Changing Magic of Not
Giving a Fuck*, 10, 110, 141,
148, 247
mental health and, 186, 188–89
No Fucks Given Guides of, 10–11,
13, 75, 99, 136, 148
Power Poses used by, 125–26
resourcefulness of roommate of,
168
TEDx Talk of, 10, 125, 247
tidiness of, 250
at tire blowouts, 173
tweeting of professional grievance,
114–15
You Do You, 10, 68
knowing your limits, 166

letting it go, 122–23
*Life-Changing Magic of Not Giving a
Fuck, The* (Knight), 10, 110,
141, 148, 247
likability, 100–102
limitations, 166
listmaking, 202–3
lying, 80–81, 239

"Magic of Not Giving a F*ck, The"
    (Knight), 125–26
"Make believe and make it work"
    exercise, 171–72
making shit happen, 157–60
making sucky things suck less,
    59–60, 64
manners, 16, 34. *See also* politeness
Master Equivocators, 239–40
maturity, 17, 18, 70
MDM (Must-Do Method), 207–8
MDM (Must-Do Method) 2.0,
    208–10
meetings
    showing up late to, 240
    taking minutes for, 169
mental health, 186–91
menu options, 154–55
mind-set about apologizing, 243–45
mistakes, admitting, 237–42
moisturizer, 176
money, dealing with, 214–23
    critical thinking in, 216, 217
    prioritizing in, 216, 217–18, 220
    resourcefulness in, 216, 222
    saving, 61, 219–21
mortgages, 222
multiple jobs, holding down, 218–19
Must-Do Method (MDM), 207–8
Must-Do Method (MDM) 2.0,
    208–10

needs, honestly assessing and
    expressing, 89–91
neighbors, apologizing to, 246

No Fucks Given Guides, 10–11, 13,
    75, 99, 136, 148
nonmonetary resources, 218
NotSorry Method, 247

"one third, two thirds" policy, 220,
    221
optimizing, 57–58, 64
orchestrate outcomes, 41–44
"Out of Office" delay tactic, 118–22
overcommitting, 195–96, 206–7
owning up, 229–48
    apologizing and, 242–48
    constructive criticism and, 230–37
    when you fucked up, 237–42

packing cubes, 199
parents
    boundaries laid down by, 136–37,
        138
    teachings of, 15–16
planning in advance, 193–95,
    199–201, 204–7
please, alternatives to, 105
poise, maintaining, 124–27
politeness, 99–100
    alternatives to please, 105
    alternatives to thank you, 107
    alternatives to you're welcome,
        111
    likability and, 100–102
    respectability and, 102–3
    ways to be polite, 104–13
Power Poses, 125–26, 230
Presence (Cuddy), 125

prioritizing, 148–49
  in dealing with money stuff, 216, 217–18, 220
  dependability and, 207–10
  values and, 149, 150–51
privilege, 92–97, 130, 215
proactive mind-set, embracing, 164–65

race, 93, 95, 215
reading the room, 135–36
refinancing mortgages, 222
relationships. *See* family; friends; parents; romantic partners
relief
  in addressing mental health issues, 191
  anticipating and orchestrating in, 43
  of being Total Fucking Grownups, 36–37, 40
rent, 112, 165, 240
renters insurance, 253
repetition and habits, 62–63
resourcefulness, 166–73
  in dealing with money stuff, 216, 222
  "Make believe and make it work" exercise for, 171–72
  "saving humanity" angle of, 170
respect
  GTFU MO and, 18
  likability and, 102
  for other people's boundaries, 76, 136–41
  politeness and, 102–3
  self-control and, 129–31

responsibility, 70
  acting responsibly. *See* dependability
  for mental health, 186–91
  as part of GTFU MO, 17, 18
  for physical health, 174–81
    alcohol habits and, 178–79
    first aid supplies and, 183
    getting and going to a doctor, 183–85
    no one-size fits-all prescription for, 175–76
    other people's notions and, 181–82
    sexual health and, 177–78
    sleep and, 177
  taking on. *See* independence
Reverse ABC, 258–62
rewards
  in addressing mental health issues, 191
  anticipating and orchestrating, 43
  for being Total Fucking Grownups, 33–36, 40
ringworm, 185
romantic partners
  apologizing to, 246
  asking for wants and needs from, 90–91
  bonding with, 134
  boundaries of, 138, 139
  communicating with, 87, 90–91, 128, 132–33
  criticism from, 232, 233, 236
  honesty with, 87, 90–91, 128

romantic partners *(cont.)*
   respectfully listening to, 103
   stepping up after ignoring
      expressed needs of, 252–53
   whining to, 132–33
roommates
   honesty with, 78
   politeness towards, 106, 107
   showing respect during financial
      problems with, 130
RSVPs, 110

sale weekends, 214
Saran Wrap, 262
"saving humanity" angle of
      resourcefulness, 170
self-awareness, 77
   about privilege, 92–97, 130
   honesty and, 79, 80–84, 87,
      89–91, 135
   and knowing your limits, 166
   three-step path toward, 79–86
self-control, 98
   articulateness and, 127–29
   coping and, 113–16
   poise and, 124–27
   politeness and, 99–113
   in saving money, 219
   self-soothing techniques and,
      116–23, 230
      just fucking let it go, 122–23
      putting yourself in "time-out,"
         117–18, 122
      triple O, 118–22
   and showing respect, 129–31

self-soothing techniques,
      116–23
self-sufficiency, 158–60, 166
sex and sexual activities, 139
sexual health, 177–78
sexuality as limiting access,
      93, 94
sheets, fitted, 262
shoes, resoling, 213–14
shopping, grocery, 158, 159, 160
significant others. *See* romantic
      partners
silence, 104–7
Slack channel, 106, 130
sleep
   deprivation, 81, 82, 83, 86
   improving, 177
smartphones, 257
snacks, 85
social media, 96
socioeconomic status as limiting
      access, 93
solving for x, 58–59, 64
speeding, 240
spirit animal, 97
stepping up, 249–55

taking minutes for meetings, 169
talking the talk, 89–91
taxes
   freelancing and, 221
   preparing, 64, 221
texts, 111, 158
TFGs. *See* Total Fucking Grownups
      (TFGs)

thank you
    alternatives to, 107
    notes or texts, 111
Theoretical Adults, 28–29, 32–33, 45,
        199, 241–42, 251
    apologizing and, 244
    consequences and, 39, 42–43
    dependability of, 193, 212
    in evolution of Total Fucking
        Grownups, 26
    fear of making "wrong" decisions,
        152
    initiative and, 162
    job interviews and, 47, 49–50,
        52–53
    lateness and, 204
    Must-Do Method (MDM) and,
        207–8
    reaction to criticism, 233
    self-sufficiency of, 158, 159
time-outs, 117–18, 122
time zones, 257
timeliness, 204–7, 240
tires, knowing how to change, 173
toilet seats, 173
Total Fucking Grownups (TFGs), 29,
        165, 265–66
    apologizing and, 243, 245
    consequences and, 38–44
    dependability of, 192, 204, 211,
        212
    evolution of, 26, 54
    first step toward becoming, 37–40
    flowchart, 71, 264
    job interviews and, 47–48, 50, 53

making effort to become, reason
        for, 32–33
    owning up to mistakes, 238, 241
    politeness and, 104, 105, 107, 111
    prioritizing and, 151–52
    qualities of, 32
    reaction to criticism, 231–32, 236
    rejecting pressure to conform, 181
    resourcefulness of, 170–71, 173
    as respecting other people's
        boundaries, 136
    rewards for being, 33–36, 40
    self-sufficiency of, 158, 166
    as stepping up, 251
travel
    long car trips and using the
        bathroom, 263–64
    packing cubes for, 199
    planning, 160, 212
    politeness and, 102
triple O technique, 118–22
Twitter, 114–15
two things being true at the same
        time, 234–35

vacation planning, 160, 212
value-based decisions, 148–52

walking the walk, 89–91
wants, honesty about, 89–91
wardrobe choices, 154, 156
warranties, 213
weddings, 236
whining, 131–35
Why the Fuck Not, 6n

work
    deadlines at, 112
    getting caught after sneaking out
        early from, 239
    politeness at, 101, 106–7
    stepping up after error at, 251–52
    taking minutes for meeting at, 169
    See also bosses; colleagues
work ethic, 15

"world clock" feature on
        smartphones, 257

You Do You, 10, 68
You-Tube videos, 170
you're welcome, alternatives
        to, 111

zit cream, 61

About the Author

Sarah Knight's first book, *The Life-Changing Magic of Not Giving a Fuck,* has been published in more than thirty languages, and her TEDx talk, "The Magic of Not Giving a F*ck," has more than ten million views. Many of the books in her No Fucks Given Guides series have been international bestsellers, including *Get Your Shit Together,* which was on the *New York Times* bestseller list for sixteen weeks. After quitting her corporate job in 2015 to pursue a freelance life, she moved from Brooklyn, New York, to the Dominican Republic, where she currently resides with her husband and two rescue cats: Gladys Knight and Mister Stussy.

You can learn more and sign up for her newsletter at sarah knight.com, and follow Sarah on Instagram, Facebook, and Tik-Tok @sarahknightauthor or on Twitter @MCSnugz.

Also Available

Praise for Sarah Knight

"Genius." — *Cosmopolitan*

"Self-help to swear by." — *Boston Globe*

"Hilarious and truly practical." — *Booklist*